THE THIN MAN IN THE CHERRY ORCHARD

THE THIN MAN IN
THE CHERRY ORCHARD

Bambi Everson

EVERSON
COLEMAN

NEW YORK

AUTHOR'S NOTE

Nick and Nora are the perfect sophisticated couple. They drink a lot but should never appear drunk (hung over, yes, but never drunk). Their banter with each other is teasing and light hearted, never angry. They speak in the quick, snappy mode of 1940s screwball comedies, in direct contrast to the Chekovian characters, but they clearly adore each other.

My love of film began at a young age. I had seen the entire THIN MAN series by the time I was ten. I was drawn to Nick and Nora's witty banter and playful teasing. Never harsh. Always with love. I wanted to be Myrna Loy when I grew up, but I wound up more like Zasu Pitts.

In 2014, I went back to school after a 37 year absence. It was in Lynda Crawford's Playwriting Lab, that I met David Logan Rankin. His dulcet tones brought old school Hollywood flooding back to me, and I knew I wanted to write something for him. I also had the privilege of meeting Wynne Anders, who was classy and exquisite in everything she did. When I studied Chekhov in Lucy Winner's Theater History class, the idea came to me like a bolt of lightning on a religious shrine, and THE THIN MAN IN THE CHERRY ORCHARD began its journey. I was honored to have both David and Wynne with me from its inception. David was instrumental in bringing this play to The Metropolitan Playhouse and for that I owe him a debt of gratitude.

Special thanks to Lynda Crawford, Lucy Winner, Virginia Urban, Suzanne Savoy, and Sidney Fortner. Props were provided by The Edward Urban estate. Other props and emotional support courtesy of Michael Aschner.

I want to acknowledge my wonderful cast and director who took this play off the page and breathed life into it; my partner in life and art, Frank Coleman, who makes things happen; and all of you, because without you, our audience, theater simply cannot exist.

Bambi Everson
New York City, July 2021

THE THIN MAN in
THE CHERRY ORCHARD

EVERSON
COLEMAN

BAMBI EVERSON

ORIGINAL PRODUCTION

The world premiere of THE THIN MAN IN THE CHERRY ORCHARD was at The Metropolitan Playhouse, 220 East Fourth Street, NYC (Alex Roe, Artistic Director), as part of the New York International Fringe Festival, October 17 - 20, 2019.

CAST
David Logan Rankin* - Nick Charles
Elizabeth Ruelas* - Nora Charles
Wynne Anders* - Madame Ranevskaya
Becca Kaplan - Anya
Cole Lamison - Varya
Byron O'Hanlon - Peter
Cameron Bossert - Simon
Dan Haft* - Inspector Ivanovich

*Equity Members appearing with permission of Actors' Equity Association without benefit of an Equity contract in this Off-Off Broadway production.

Production Stage Manager - Rebecca Kaplan
Lights - Leslie Gray
Sound Design - Frank Coleman

Directed by Job Ethan Christenson
An Everson/Coleman Production

David Logan Rankin, Becca Kaplan, Byron O'Hanlon, Cole Lamison, Wynne Anders, Elizabeth Ruelas, Cameron Bossert (l to r). Not pictured: Dan Haft. Photo: F. Coleman.

THE THIN MAN IN THE CHERRY ORCHARD
By Bambi Everson

Approximately 100 minutes
with one optional intermission

CHARACTERS:

MADAME (MME) RANEVSKAYA (50s) - Matriarch of the family.
Elegant and refined in appearance. She is a spendthrift, and dirt poor, but
wants to hold on to any shred of dignity left in her.

ANYA RANEVSKAYA (20s) - MME. RANEVSKAYA's youngest
daughter. Hopeful, impulsive.

VARYA RANEVSKAYA (20s) - MME. RANEVSKAYA's adopted
daughter, a few years older than ANYA. Anxious, protective.

PETER TROVIMOV (30s) - Perpetual student and philosopher. Former
tutor to MME. RANEVSKAYA's son and former paramour of ANYA.

SIMON SMIRNOV (30s) - Caretaker of Cherry manor. Overworked,
anxious and slightly bitter. Secretly in love with VARYA.

NICK CHARLES (40s) - The world famous detective. Witty and urbane.
Devoted to his wife.

NORA CHARLES (40s) - A charming and witty sophisticate.
Independently wealthy and madly in love with her husband.

INSPECTOR IVANOVICH (40s-50s) - Career law enforcement officer.
Ineffectual, arrogant and stiff.

PLACE: A suburb in Russia, not too far from Moscow.
TIME: 1940s.

SYNOPSIS:

In this sardonic parody, Dashiell Hammet's hard-boiled, glamorously pickled American sleuths, Nick and Nora Charles, meet their cousins, the stoic inhabitants of Chekhov's bleak Russian tundra. Naturally, a murder, and hilarity, ensues. Can Nick solve the crime before they run out of vodka?

SETS AND LIGHTING:

Single interior set; Most of the action takes place in a living room; Lighting changes should suffice for two scenes, an outdoor bench and the interior of a train compartment.

SCENE LIST

SCENE 1 - Living room of the Cherry Manor Home
SCENE 2 - The interior of a train compartment
SCENE 3 - Early morning in Cherry Manor
SCENE 4 - A few hours later
SCENE 5 - Later that afternoon
SCENE 6 - A bench outside the house
SCENE 7 - In the dining area
SCENE 8 - The next morning
SCENE 9 - Moments later
SCENE 10 - A few minutes later

NOTE: In the original production of THIN MAN, we opted not to include an intermission. Future productions may want to, so we've indicated in the script where that should be, if so. When resuming, pick up the action right where you left off.

SCENE 1

OPENING MONTAGE

These notes are based on the choreography by director Job Ethan Christenson for the original production at The Metropolitan Playhouse in 2019. Consider them a guide, not a strict set of orders. Future productions should feel free to adapt them to suit their needs and purposes.

The idea is to portray something like a cinematic montage to introduce the characters and set the mood, alternating between the Ranevskaya mansion, and a train station.

Suggested music: Jack Hylton - Life is Just a Bowl of Cherries (1931).

Blackout. NICK appears, center stage, wearing a trench coat and fedora, with his back to the audience. He flicks open his 1940s cigarette lighter with its signature metallic ching, and lights a cigarette. The flame from the lighter is the only illumination on stage at first, then a spotlight from above fades in on NICK as he exhales a large puff of smoke, permeating the stage. NICK snaps the lighter shut, turns towards the audience, checks his watch, looks around for NORA, pulls a newspaper out of his pocket, sticks his nose in it and starts to leave. The headline is about him cracking a case. NORA enters, crosses to NICK and slaps the paper down to get his attention. They smile at each other, NICK gallantly takes NORA's arm and they exit. Lights fade.

Lights up on the dining area of the Ranevskaya house. SIMON enters and begins straightening up the place settings. Pours himself a cup of coffee. PETER enters, unceremoniously takes the cup for himself, ignoring SIMON's angry stare, and exits.

SIMON continues to straighten up. VARYA enters. SIMON crosses to meet her and help her out of her coat, but ends up twisting her arms a little, which annoys her slightly. SIMON takes her coat sheepishly and exits. VARYA exits in the opposite direction. Lights fade.

Lights up on ANYA as she enters, wearing a heavy coat and carrying a suitcase. She hurriedly crosses, looking for her train, and exits. Lights fade.

Lights up on NORA as she enters, a suitcase in one hand, a picnic basket in the other. NICK enters close behind her, his nose in his newspaper, taking occasional slugs from his hip flask. NORA stops, and holds out her arms to signal NICK to take the bags. He ignores her and strides past, his nose still in his paper. NORA unceremoniously drops the suitcase to the floor with a bang to get his attention. Smiling indulgently and solicitously, NICK hurries back to her and picks up the suitcase, as NORA crosses in front of him, her nose in the air, still carrying the picnic basket, and exits. NICK dutifully follows close behind.

LIGHTS AND MUSIC FADE. END OF MONTAGE.

Lights up on the living room of the Cherry Manor Home. It is decorated like a cheap facsimile of a Victorian home. There is a sidebar against one wall with alcohol in decanters, plush armchairs (slightly frayed) and a sofa that has seen better days. There is a large, nearly empty bookcase filled with tacky knickknacks, snow globes, souvenirs, and a photo of the owner, Mr. Yepikov, in better days. There is a window that looks out on the guest cottages, pool, and the barren cherry orchard, but it is pitch black at night, only visible during the daytime scenes. At opening, VARYA is examining the room. She is clearly anxious, fixing her hair, and pacing. SIMON is setting up the bar. There is a tense silence for a few moments.

VARYA
So where is he?

SIMON
How should I know? The telegram said he was arriving yesterday. Typical. I knocked myself out making this place presentable!

VARYA
How long has it looked like this?

SIMON
After a couple of years, the dirt doesn't get any worse. This is too much
for one person to manage, you know. Your fiancé fled like a rat from a
sinking ship.

VARYA
(starts cleaning)
He's NOT my fiancé!

SIMON
Sorry.

VARYA
Don't mention it.

SIMON
It's just that everyone expected that you two...

VARYA
I said don't mention it! Why do people keep bringing it up?
(pause)
I'm fine now. I'm absolutely fine!

SIMON
Sorry.

VARYA
He's the one who should be sorry. I waited for him to make his move. He
literally watched me pack my bags. I gave him every opportunity. He just
stood there like a monk who had taken a vow of silence.

SIMON
(sighing)
That's despicable, really.

VARYA

All this time, I have been less than 50 miles away. Don't push, they said. No one likes an aggressive female. He's just gun-shy. But for a woman, the years slip away quickly.

SIMON

You look more lovely than ever, Ms. Varya.
(catching himself)
Mr. Yepikov is going to regret losing you.

VARYA

What? Did he say anything? Has he mentioned me? He knows I'm coming back right?

SIMON

No. No. And yes.

VARYA

Well, I don't care. I am just here for Mama and Anya.

SIMON

You have some dirt on your forehead.

VARYA hurriedly rubs it off and checks herself.

VARYA

Weren't they supposed to be on the evening train? It's getting late.

SIMON

Relax. They should be here any minute. Traffic is worse than ever since they put the highway in. No one takes this road anymore. No one remembers.

VARYA

Any minute? Oh, she can't see it like this. What happened to the carpeting?

SIMON
I sold the carpets to an antique dealer from Minsk just to keep the gas on.

VARYA
Good heavens! Hand me that cloth. At least I can get rid of these cobwebs.

SIMON
Don't kill the spiders.

VARYA
(*starts tidying*)
You have all of us for company now, Simon. What happened to the tenants?

SIMON
Gone. I couldn't afford to heat the cottages so they've been empty for some time. Everything fell to me. When Yepikov let Peter live here, I was afraid I was going to be let go, but no, Peter is just another mouth for me to feed.

VARYA
Ugh! Peter! He's always been a freeloader! But maybe Gregor - I mean, Mr. Yepikov - sees the error of his ways. Maybe he wants to give Cherry Manor back to us!

SIMON
It's all very confusing. Yepikov just asked that we all get together for the holidays. Rather short notice, if you ask me. I was going mad from boredom, so I invited my American cousin, Nora, and her husband here for a visit. They were well on their way when I got word from Yepikov. I don't know how we'll manage.

VARYA
Simon! You never told any of us about your family. I always assumed you just grew here. Part of the landscape.

SIMON

You never asked. I lived in America until I was 14. Nora is my mother's brother's child. Old money from his wife's side. They're rolling in it. Nora and I were very close as children, She had this je ne sais quoi. A devil-may-care attitude, even at ten. She inherited buckets of money but apparently she - um... married beneath herself. An amateur detective of sorts. Drinks like a fish. Caused quite the scandal.

VARYA

Not everyone grows up with the same values they had as a child.

SIMON

Nora did. We've kept up correspondence. She's still a pip.

VARYA

Being fabulously wealthy doesn't hurt, either.

SIMON

Well... yes. That fact did not escape me. So please, be nice to the both of them. Especially her deadbeat husband. She worships him. Heaven knows why. This means NO flirting, Varya. Keep those feminine wiles of yours under wraps, for once.

VARYA

Oh Simon, you spoil all my fun.

The door flings open. ANYA enters with suitcases. MME. RANEVSKAYA is close behind. ANYA drops her bags and runs to VARYA.

ANYA

We're here! We made it! Oh, Varya. It's so good to see you. Let me look at you. Oh, it's been too long! And you, Simon...
(hugs him quickly and tentatively)
Would you help Mama with the bags?

SIMON

Certainly. Welcome home, Madame Ranevskaya.

MME. RANEVSKAYA steps in, gasping at the sight of things.

MME. RANEVSKAYA
Home? You call this home? I have no home! I have been living like an animal for months. The jungle is my home!

ANYA
(hugging her mother)
Oh Mama - such histrionics! Paris wasn't exactly the jungle.

MME. RANEVSKAYA
Oh, my sweet child. You have no idea. You were off in school. You don't know what I endured. Whatever possessed me to return to that beast?

VARYA
We warned you, Mama, but you felt there was no option after... Never mind, you're here now. That's what matters. I've missed you so.
(hugs her)
Please sit down. Can I get you a drink?

MME. RANEVSKAYA
(examining the room with great distaste)
Yes. I shall need one. I am guessing it's the maid's day off?

She dusts the sofa with her handkerchief. ANYA is looking around nostalgically.

VARYA
(brings a drink)
Oh, Mama. I know it looks bad.

MME. RANEVSKAYA
Bad? Kafka would find it too depressing!

ANYA
It just needs a little sprucing up, Mama. Some new curtains, a coat of paint.

MME. RANEVSKAYA
It's like sitting on a memory. And flattening it beyond recognition.

SIMON returns with many suitcases under his arms. No one offers to help.

SIMON
I'll put you in your old room shall I, Madame? And Anya - is the nursery all right? Varya has settled in the second bedroom.

MME. RANEVSKAYA
(distracted)
Yes. Fine.

ANYA
(also distracted)
Thank you.

MME. RANEVSKAYA looks around, disgusted.

VARYA
Mama, I have a feeling things are going to turn out all right. After all, why would Gregor– I mean, Mr. Yepikov… invite us here after all this time? Maybe he's ready to do what he should have done in the first place.

MME. RANEVSKAYA
I don't trust Gregor to do anything that doesn't benefit Gregor. The man has stabbed me in the back before. Where is he? I am exhausted.

VARYA
Simon thought he should have arrived by now. He'll probably be on the next train.

MME. RANEVSKAYA
I wait for no man. I am turning in. I hope someone has aired out the sheets.

She stares at SIMON, who has recently returned.

MME. RANEVSKAYA
Anya?

ANYA
In a minute, Mama.

MME. RANEVSKAYA
Simon, will there be coffee in the morning? You know how unpleasant I can be without my morning coffee.

SIMON
Everything will be as you wish, Madame. It is good to have you home again.

MME. RANEVSKAYA
Yes. The reception has been quite touching.

MME. RANEVSKAYA exits upstairs.

SIMON
The marching band was on hiatus.

ANYA
You had to expect she would react that way. It is an awful shock.

SIMON
Get ready for another one. Peter's here too!

ANYA
Peter? Where?

SIMON
He's been staying in one of the guest cottages finishing one of his many dissertations on the meaninglessness of life. Shall I go wake him?

ANYA
No. I look awful.

VARYA
Let him sleep. It's the one thing he's been successful at. Well, that and eating our food. You will see him at breakfast, darling. Let's go upstairs. I'll help you unpack and you can tell me all about your adventures.

ANYA
Goodnight, Simon. You won't forget Mama's coffee, will you?

SIMON
I'll see to it all now. Goodnight, ladies.

Ladies exit. SIMON watches them go, then goes to the bar and pours himself a stiff drink. He looks out at the darkened cherry orchard.

SIMON
Fasten your seatbelts. It's going to be a bumpy ride.
(takes a drink)

BLACKOUT

SCENE 2

Suggested transition music: Ronnie Munro - Me & My Girl (1938).

The interior of a train compartment. NICK and NORA are sitting across from each other. NORA is eating a sandwich. NICK is hidden behind a newspaper, pretending to read.

NORA
Sandwich, Nicky?
(he ignores her)
Blini?
(offers him a bottle)
Tarkun?
(grabs his paper away)
Oh, for goodness sake, Nicky. Stop sulking.

NICK
(grabs paper back)
I am not sulking! I just don't happen to like mysterious brown meat and onions. It doesn't become you, either.

NORA takes a drink, gargles a bit, then comes over and kisses him.

NORA
Is this better?

NICK
(kisses her back for a moment)
Hmmm... reminds me that I miss our dog!

NORA
Oh, Nicky! You know we couldn't possibly bring Asta. He would have to be quarantined for months.

NICK
So instead, I'm quarantined. I really don't see why we needed to make

NICK (cont.)

this ridiculous journey. The plane was insufferable. Watered down drinks and ugly stewardesses, and now three days on this Godforsaken train... sleeping in those bunks... I feel like the china plates we only use when your mother visits.

NORA

We needed to get far away, Nicky. You almost got killed back there!

NICK

I was merely pushing the envelope, my dear Mrs. Charles.

NORA

You were lucky. If I hadn't hit that man on the head with my tray of canapés, you might have been pushing up daisies! Honestly, Nicky, the people you invite for dinner!

NICK

He's been sent up the river for 20 years, darling. Out of sight, out of mind. I don't know why we needed to be exiled to Siberia as well...

NORA

I haven't seen my cousin Simon since we were children.

NICK

If he's like the rest of your family, that might be fortuitous.

NORA

Well, I remember him fondly. I always say, "Never judge a book by it's mother." Simon never had the disadvantage of being spoiled by wealth... like some people. I wish we didn't have to travel all the way to Russia for a little R and R, but at least we won't risk running into any of your nefarious adversaries.

NICK

I can't help it if I am sought after, my dear. Lucky for you, you reeled me in.

NORA

And I don't intend to cut you loose again.

(kisses him)

A couple of weeks in the middle of nowhere will be good for us. No doorbells ringing in the middle of the night. No mysterious women from your past popping up, desperate for help. Just you and me, quiet moonlit nights, nothing more exciting than a game of Scrabble.

NICK

Last time you hit me with your shoe when I got 300 points for "QUETZALS." You realize, Russian Scrabble has 104 alphabet tiles. We won't even know what we are spelling. But I do like the idea of you in the moonlight, Mrs. Charles.

NORA

Simon has been making his own brand of cherry vodka for years. I bet if you behave yourself, he'll let you sample some.

NICK

Why didn't you say that in the first place, darling?

(takes out his flask)

To you, my dark-haired enchantress and the ineffable pleasure of drinking at someone else's expense. You always make mouth-watering decisions. Onward Ho!

Train sounds and Russian patriotic music, such as the Red Army choir, plays as the lights fade.

BLACKOUT

SCENE 3

Early morning in Cherry Manor. Everything is bright and sunny in contrast to last night. The picture window now shows the barren cherry orchard and the edge of a swimming pool that has not been in use for some time. At the opening, PETER is standing by the table, which has a samovar filled with hot coffee. Fixings, cups, plates, and saucers are on the table as is an assortment of baked goods. SIMON is arranging the table.

PETER
(eating)
The bread's a little stale, Simon.

SIMON
Well, with everything going on, I didn't exactly have time to bake, now did I? Put some jam on it, and for God's sake, don't say anything to Madame Ranevskaya.

PETER
Maybe you can take a drive into town later. I need a new typewriter ribbon. And it's pretty chilly in the guesthouse, perhaps I should move into the main house.

SIMON
Oh, sure. You and everyone else. Anything else I can do for you? Change the scenery? Wallpaper the outhouse toolshed? Fill the tub with champagne?

MME. RANEVSKAYA enters, grandly clutching her head.

MME. RANEVSKAYA
No champagne! Coffee. Just coffee. My head is splitting.

SIMON
Right away, Madame Ranevskaya.
(pours coffee, lots of sugar)

PETER
Madame Ranevskaya.
(goes to kiss her hand)

MME. RANEVSKAYA
Peter. You look...

PETER
Older?
(laughs)

MME. RANEVSKAYA
No. I was going to say... different. You cleaned yourself up a bit.

PETER
I've been studying in Paris. Spinozist Elements in Jean Paul Sartre's "Being and Nothingness."

MME. RANEVSKAYA gets her coffee from SIMON.

MME. RANEVSKAYA
(sarcastically)
Riveting.

ANYA enters.

ANYA
Do I smell coffee?
(pause... coldly)
Hello, Peter.

PETER
Anya!
(runs to her)
You look beautiful. You have blossomed like a flower.

ANYA

You never leave your room. How would you even know what a flower looks like?

PETER

I deserve that. I've been a monster. I felt my writing was the only weapon I had against the scourge of society. But now–

ANYA

You're eating your words?

PETER

The last time we saw each other, I was filled with intolerable despair. There was nothing to live by, and nothing to live for. I felt like I was going to vanish. My thoughts, my very soul, dust scattered to the winds.

ANYA

Forever the poet. But even Alexander Pushkin found time for love. Actions speak louder than words, Peter. Your only action was silence. How long was I supposed to wait? What was I even waiting for?

PETER

Pushkin was a hack! He was the bourgeois! What did he know about human suffering? I suffered for my art.

SIMON

And now it's our turn.

PETER

Things will be different from here on in. Anya, you will see. Now I see doors where I used to see walls.

ANYA

Some doors might be slammed in your face and on your foot! Repeatedly.

PETER
Closed, but hopefully not locked. I remember a time when you felt
differently...

*He goes to kiss her. She resists for a second, but yields to him. Then pulls
away. She is conflicted. The front doorbell rings.*

MME. RANEVSKAYA
It's too early in the day for this nonsense. Especially on an empty
stomach. Anya, Come eat your breakfast. Simon, the door!

SIMON opens the front door. NICK and NORA enter with suitcases.

NICK
Good heavens. I thought we'd never get here alive.

PETER
(pouring a quick drink from the bar)
Have a drink.

NICK
(dropping everything)
I thought you'd never ask.

NORA
Simon, darling!
(hugs him)
Oh, it's been so long.

SIMON
I would never have recognized you.

NICK
Yes. The plastic surgeon did a magnificent job. Last week, she looked
like Eleanor Roosevelt.

NORA
Oh, Nicky! Don't be ridiculous. Simon– my husband. Mr. Nick Charles.

PETER
THE Nick Charles? The detective?

NICK
The one and only.

PETER
Peter Trovimov. I read about your case in Paris. It made page six.

NICK
Imagine that, darling... Did you hear?

NORA
I heard. But he's not doing any more detecting, are you, dear?

NICK
No, that avenue of pleasure has been shut down. Presently, my main pursuit is taking care of my wife's money.

NORA
And he is rather expert in that field.

MME. RANEVSKAYA
This bread is stale... FIRS!!!!
(silence)

ANYA
Mama! Firs has been gone for some time now. Don't you remember?
(turns to NORA apologetically)
Firs was our servant.

SIMON
Firs is still with us, Madame.

ANYA
Of course, Always in our hearts.

SIMON
No. He's literally still with us. I buried him in the back yard.

ANYA
Oh, my God! Poor Firs...

SIMON
Poor me! I was the one who found him. Sitting in that chair. Staring at
the cherry orchard. He had been there for days. His arm literally adhered
to the chair. When I lifted him up, his skin came off like a glove. You'll
notice I had it reupholstered. Worse than that, the ground was frozen
solid. I had to wait until spring for the ground to thaw. He spent the
winter in the tool shed.

NORA
How awful. You couldn't call someone?

SIMON
Firs spent his life here. He had no family. He'd been forgotten by
everyone. I figured he wouldn't want to be anywhere else. So he's there. I
planted one cherry tree right by the pool. It just began to flower last
spring... Good fertilizer.

MME. RANEVSKAYA
Pool? There's a pool?
(runs to the window)
Oh, how could you?

SIMON
I had to do something to appease the summer tenants. Once they put the
highway in, it was impossible to get to the river.

MME. RANEVSKAYA
This is a pool? It looks like a swamp.

SIMON
It hasn't been in use since the last tenants left. That was two years ago. I should have drained it, but toads began breeding there and I liked the sound.

MME. RANEVSKAYA
Oh, I can't bear it. I am not going to look at that foul bog for another minute. After what happened to my boy...

ANYA
(to NICK)
My brother Grisha drowned in the river, many years ago. I don't think Mama's ever gotten over it.

NICK
I can't imagine anyone would. Come, have a drink, Madame Ranevskaya.
(pours her one)

MME. RANEVSKAYA
I never drink before 4.

NICK
Pity.
(downs the drink himself)

SIMON
I'll cover the pool immediately, Madame. We'll drain it later. Can I get some assistance, gentlemen?

PETER
What about all the toads?

SIMON
We'll leave one corner untied. I am sure they'll find their way out. I spotted a Siberian salamander last week. Fascinating creatures. Their bodies are filled with something resembling anti-freeze to combat the cold. Some have been frozen for years and just walk off once they thaw.

PETER
(breaking the spell)
Coming, Mr. Charles?

NICK
I have an aversion to reptiles and assorted slimy things.

NORA
That's odd considering the company you have been keeping lately. I'll
help.

NICK
Coming, dear. I'll just put away this liquor.

He takes another drink. The men and NORA exit.

MME. RANEVSKAYA
Finish your breakfast, Anya. What is keeping Varya? Did that
phlegmatic Mr. Yepikov make an appearance yet? He certainly has some
explaining to do.

ANYA
I don't think she slept well last night, Mama. I heard her pacing about.
I'm sure she's anxious about seeing Mr. Yepikov. You don't suppose she
still carries a torch, do you?

MME. RANEVSKAYA
Only to set him on fire! He's a swine. And your Peter isn't much better.
Still a ubiquitous loafer.

ANYA
There seems to be something different about him. He seems transformed
somehow.

MME. RANEVSKAYA
Yes, but into what? Ah, here comes the late Varya Ranevskaya now.

MME. RANEVSKAYA (cont.)
(to VARYA)
Hurry, dear, before the coffee gets cold.

VARYA enters in a flurry. She has her hair done and looks like she has done herself up well intentionally.

VARYA
Sorry I'm late, mama. Where is everyone?

MME. RANEVSKAYA
HE has not materialized yet. Everyone else is out by the... pool.

VARYA
(grabbing some bread and a cup of coffee)
...The pool?

She runs out. ANYA and MME. RANEVSKAYA exchange a knowing glance and then proceed to pour themselves more coffee and eat their breakfast.

Silence... Then an earth-shattering scream from VARYA! She rushes in through the French doors, followed by PETER.

VARYA
He's dead! He's dead! Oh, my God! Oh, my God! He's dead!

MME. RANEVSKAYA
Calm down, child. I didn't get a chance to tell you. Firs died some time ago and we only just found out ourselves. A shock, I know, but not unexpected.

VARYA
What are you talking about? Not Firs! It's Gregor! My Gregor!

ANYA
What are you saying?

She starts to run outside. PETER stops her.

PETER
Don't look. It's Mr. Yepikov, MME. He must have fallen into the pool.

ANYA and MME. RANEVSKAYA look towards the door. All we see are two boots and the legs of a man. SIMON and NICK are covering him with the pool cover. SIMON enters, then NICK and NORA.

SIMON
How horribly tragic. We thought there was this large turtle in the pool, but on closer inspection we saw it was wearing an overcoat. Poor Yepikov. He must have wandered in from the back and lost his footing. I must notify the authorities. I will use the kitchen phone. Excuse me. This is most disturbing.

SIMON walks off stage.

MME. RANEVSKAYA
The scoundrel was probably drunk. Every Christmas, he would put away an entire bottle of our best cognac. He was useless.

VARYA
Oh Mama! How could you? I know Gregor wasn't much, but he was all I had. Now I will go to my grave without ever knowing the love of a man. No one will want me now. I am nearly 30.

She runs upstairs crying.

ANYA
(*running after VARYA*)
Honestly, Mama. Sometimes you really put your foot in it.

MME. RANEVSKAYA
I don't understand it. Gregor and I grew up together. He was on the swim team. Even drunk he could swim rings around anyone.

NICK
That would have been rather difficult – with a bullet in his back!

NORA, SIMON, MME. RANEVSKAYA and PETER gasp!

BLACKOUT

SCENE 4

Suggested transition music: Ella Logan - Oh Dear! What Can The Matter Be? (1938).

A few hours later. Everyone has gathered in the living room. Food and drinks are on the sidebar. They sit in silence.

MME. RANEVSKAYA
Well, what are we supposed to do now?

ANYA
The police said to wait, Mama. For the coroner's report.

MME. RANEVSKAYA
Why? He was dead, wasn't he? We all saw that.

NICK
The police think it must have been an intruder. But since none of us heard a shot, we need to establish the time of death. We don't know how long he'd been in the water, but it was long enough for the toads to have a nice meal.

NORA
Must you be so graphic, Nicky? There are ladies present. I think we all need a drink.

NICK
I second that. Simon, might you honor us with your cherry vodka? I've heard it's the stuff of legends.

SIMON
It's in the wine cellar. I am assuming its safe to go down there?

VARYA
I don't think we can assume anything. That maniac could still be out there. Peter, you go with him.

PETER
Sure, you'd like that. You always found me dispensable. Come on, then.
After you, Simon.

ANYA
Wait! Take my gun.

*ANYA reaches into her purse and pulls out a gun! She nonchalantly and
recklessly points the gun directly at each person as she turns to speak.
They yell in alarm (ad lib)! AAH! NO!!*

MME. RANEVSKAYA
You have a gun? Since when?

ANYA
The streets of Paris can be frightening for a woman on her own.

NICK
I'm sorry, but I'll have to ask you to hand that over. We have not found
the murder weapon yet.

ANYA
You don't think that I... Oh, this is ridiculous. Here.

She hands over the gun. NICK examines it and sniffs the barrel.

NICK
It's alright. It hasn't been fired recently. Here. Be careful.

He hands it to PETER, who exits with SIMON.

NORA
Oh Nicky, this is awful. You don't really think there was an intruder, do
you?

NICK
No, I don't. Most likely the murderer is right here in this house.

MME. RANEVSKAYA
One of us? That's preposterous. We have known Yepikov our entire
lives. If any of us had wanted to kill him, we would have had plenty of
opportunity. There was never any trouble until you showed up.

NORA
She has a point, Nicky. Trouble does seem to follow you.

NICK
Whose side are you on, anyway?

NORA
Sorry. This is going all wrong. Maybe we should have stayed in Paris,
gotten some fresh croissants and stared at The Mona Lisa. You never
hear of anyone being shot in the museum. Just once I'd like to go on
holiday without someone getting bumped off. It's getting tedious. Do
solve this quickly, Nicky. I want to do some shopping in Moscow. I need
a new hat.

SIMON and PETER enter with a bottle of cherry vodka.

SIMON
The very finest cherry vodka. Perfect for any occasion. Who wants a
shot?

ANYA
Not funny, Simon.

VARYA
I'll have a double. With olives.

PETER and SIMON begin pouring glasses of vodka for everyone.
VARYA downs hers quickly and motions for another.

SIMON
Are you imbibing, MME? The cherries are homegrown.

MME. RANEVSKAYA
Certainly not... Just put a bit in my coffee.

SIMON does.

.

MME. RANEVSKAYA (cont.)
For heavens sake, don't be so stingy! I paid for everything in this house.
Yepikov was only responsible for the mildew.

NICK
I was wondering if I might have a look around. See if Mr. Yepikov left
any clues.

SIMON
I don't see how he could. He hasn't been here for ages. Left me totally in
the lurch.

NICK
He must have been coming from somewhere. I didn't see a suitcase.
Maybe we'll find it when we drain the pool. Better get on that,
gentlemen. He wasn't on our train. Did he have a car?

VARYA
(drinking heavily)
He drove a Volga Gaz. It had a very roomy back seat. I loved that car.

Everyone looks at her knowingly.

VARYA (cont.)
Oh, what does it matter now? Oh, Gregor! Who would want to do this to
you?

SIMON
You mean besides everybody? Come on. We all know what kind of a
man he was... despite your feelings for him, which he obviously and
stupidly ignored. He ruined this house. He ruined our lives... Can any of
us honestly say we are sorry the man is gone?

MME. RANEVSKAYA
I have known him all my life. I was his protector. And then repays me by
pilfering my home. Oh, how I hate that man. Feel free to look around Mr.
Charles. If there is a knife missing, it's because he used it to stab me in
the back.

*The phone rings. No one moves. It rings a second time. Everyone yells
"SIMON!"*

SIMON
Excuse me.
(answers phone)
Cherry Manor... Yes. Hold on, please. It's for you, Mr. Charles. Inspector
Ivonovich.

NICK
Thank you.
(takes the phone)
Yes, Inspector. No, I am not here on a case... I was merely visiting...
Well, I appreciate that. Yes, I see. No... Your English is quite good.
Really... Ah, yes, as I suspected. Will do. Thank you. And regards to
Mrs. Ivonovich, if there is one. Ah... Lucky Man... No, I am happily
shackled for the time being. Well, that would be lovely after all this is
settled. The Nabikov Nitespot? That does sound intriguing. Yes. Of
course. Ha ha. Well... Do svidaniya to you, too.
(hangs up phone)
Lovely gentleman.

NORA
What did he say?

NICK
He said the Beef Stroganoff at the Nabikov Nitespot is to die for.

NORA
Really, Nicky, we're on pins and needles!

MME. RANEVSKAYA
Speak for yourself. I really have no interest in the gruesome details.

PETER
Well, I, for one, am interested. There's never been a murder in these parts before. Suicides, yes. Plenty of those around here. I mean its dreadfully dull and depressing. Who can stand it? But murder... That makes my ears prick up.

ANYA
But it had to be an intruder, no?

NICK
A very careful intruder. No footprints leading into the woods or anywhere else except the back door. Tire tracks only in one direction. Who drove up here?

VARYA
I did. I was dropped off at the foot of the hill though and walked up. I didn't see any other cars. My driver turned straight around on the gravel.

NICK
Ah. That explains the tiny holes I spotted in the grass. Your high heels, Miss Varya. Why did you come in the back way?

VARYA
I didn't... I mean, I started to, but Simon met me before I got near the cottages.

SIMON
That's true. I felt I needed to prepare her a little. I grabbed her bags and ushered her in the front. I didn't want her to see the state of things before I had a chance to...

MME. RANEVSKAYA
Is it possible a madman might still be on the premises? Simon, Go check our rooms at once! Though anyone hiding in a closet would surely be

MME. RANEVSKAYA (cont.)
asphyxiated by all the dust.

NICK
Very perplexing indeed, MME. Ranevskaya. It's unlikely that an intruder
could have entered through either door without being spotted.

SIMON
I was in all day preparing. I cleaned every room myself. I surely would
have noticed.

MME. RANEVSKAYA
Maybe you missed something. In my day, the maids would be fired for
this kind of shoddy housekeeping.

SIMON exits, insulted.

NICK
Now, now, domestic issues aside, I'm quite sure the person who shot Mr.
Yepikov is right here in the house with us. The Inspector said there was
no water in his lungs, which means he was dead approximately 12 to 18
hours when he was tossed into the pool.

NORA
Well, that lets us off, doesn't it, darling? We only arrived this morning.

NICK
Yes, dear. It appears we are the only ones in the clear. The inspector did
require that we all stay put. He will be on his way as soon as he wraps up
the paperwork.

NORA
Oh, you'll solve it by then, won't you, Nicky?
(to the others)
He really is a wonderful detective.

NICK

You forget, my little fig newton, that I am on hiatus. Imposed by you.

NORA

But this is family, Nicky. Not your usual lowlife criminals.

NICK

Ah. I see. A special breed of highbrow criminals. Murder is murder, my sweet. But, as you have lifted the iron curtain, I shall proceed. Anyone like to make a confession now? It's almost cocktail hour.

MME. RANEVSKAYA

You are indeed a repulsive man! How dare you accuse the Ranevskaya family? We come from very good stock.

NICK

Chicken or vegetable stock?
(pause)
Clearly not laughing stock. Its obvious Mr. Yepikov was not held in very high esteem by any of you.

ANYA

You are right there, Mr. Charles. But we came here hoping Mr. Yepikov had a change of heart. It wouldn't make any sense to kill him before we knew what his plans were.

NICK

Are all the other cottages locked?

PETER

All but the one I've been staying in. There's no heat, you see, but I find the brisk air invigorates my brain.

NICK

Would you mind very much if I had a look around there?

PETER
Not at all. I'll escort you.

NORA
I want to come too.

NICK
Come along then sugar. But no snooping. Brrr… It's Chilly.

NORA grabs a bottle. NICK can't see she has her fingers crossed behind her back, but we can.

NORA
Got you covered, Nicky.

As they exit, SIMON enters.

SIMON
There is no one.

MME. RANEVSKAYA
Good. I am going upstairs to take a hot bath, to wipe off the stench of that man.

ANYA
I'll run the water for you, mama. The pipes are a little rusty.

They exit. SIMON and VARYA are left alone. SIMON begins to tidy up.

SIMON
You have been conspicuously quiet.

VARYA
(pulling him aside)
I must speak with you.... My gun is missing!

SIMON
(loudly, as she tries to shush him)
WHAT!? You, too? What is it with you modern women and firearms?

VARYA
It was a gift.

SIMON
Men don't bring flowers and chocolates anymore?

VARYA
It was for my protection.

SIMON
I would have gotten a dog! You have to tell Mr. Charles.

VARYA
I will, but not just yet. Couldn't you look around again? Search Mama's bedroom while she's having her bath?

SIMON
I was just upstairs searching for a maniac, now I am searching for a murder weapon? What are you thinking?

VARYA
Mama knew I had it. She was so angry with Gregor. I wouldn't blame her for wanting to...

SIMON
Fine. I'll do it. But you have to be my lookout. What would anyone say if they saw me snooping in an old lady's bedroom?

VARYA
Just say you are airing the beds.

SIMON
And what am I supposed to do if I find it?

VARYA

Get rid of it. There is no way I'd let Mama go to prison. The woman has suffered enough. Desperate women do desperate things.

They start to go upstairs together. NICK enters.

NICK

Excuse me. Not interrupting I hope?

VARYA

Of course not, Mr. Charles. Are we out of vodka?

NICK

Good heavens, I hope not! No, I was just wondering... Did Mr. Yepikov receive any correspondence here? Maybe there is something that can shed some light on this subject.

SIMON

There is a pile in the office going back over a year now. You are welcome to rifle through it. I'll show you. Varya and I can... air the beds later. Varya, why don't you see what you can scrape together for dinner?
(to NICK)
She trained at The Cordon Blue. She makes the most marvelous turkey tetrazzini.

VARYA

You remember that?

SIMON
(tenderly)
My mouth waters at the thought.

VARYA

It's been a while, but I'll give it a shot. Oh, poor choice of words. Sorry.

SIMON

Mr. Charles, shall we?

NICK pours himself a drink.

NICK
Ah... Nectar of the Gods. Lead on, my good man.

NICK and SIMON exit. VARYA begins to search the living room. She finds a letter opener and puts it in her skirt. NORA enters and sees this.

NORA
Varya!

VARYA
A woman has the right to protect herself.

NORA
That's what Nicky is here for. I think you'd better let me take that dear. You don't want that nice inspector to find a weapon on you. Nicky always said the most dangerous woman was me in the kitchen. Maybe you can teach me something.

NORA tosses the letter opener back on the table and walks into the kitchen. VARYA follows, but turns back and grabs the letter opener and puts it back in her skirt, looking around suspiciously, before exiting behind her.

BLACKOUT

SCENE 5

Suggested transition music: Ella Fitzgerald and The Inkspots - Into Each Life Some Rain Must Fall (1944)

Late Afternoon. Everyone has gathered in the living room. ANYA is trying to read a book, but can't. PETER is finishing off the leftovers from lunch. VARYA is drying her hands with a towel. She absentmindedly leaves it on the table.

MME. RANEVSKAYA
Varya, please put that back in the kitchen. We have company coming.

VARYA
It's the police, mama. That's not exactly company.

MME. RANEVSKAYA
Simon, please tidy up the lunch table and make some fresh coffee. Anya, What are you reading?

ANYA shows her.

ANYA
"Dead Souls" by Nikolai Gogol.

MME. RANEVSKAYA
For heaven's sake, what would the police think if they saw you reading that? Go and put that upstairs at once.

ANYA
Fine.

She does.

MME. RANEVSKAYA
Peter, you could use a shave. You look decidedly unsanitary.

NORA
Mme. Ranevskaya, try to relax.

MME. RANEVSKAYA
I have been home for two days. In that time, I have seen my childhood home desecrated, a dead man floating in my backyard, my daughter taking up with a grubby loafer, and your husband depleting our liquor cabinet. Don't tell me to relax!

SIMON re-enters with coffee.

SIMON
Your coffee, Madame.

Doorbell rings. Nobody moves. ANYA runs downstairs.

NICK
I'll get it.

Finishes off his drink and prances to the door cheerily. The first lines are said offstage as the assembled parties prepare for the guest.

NICK
Inspector Ivonovich! Good afternoon. Do come in. We have touched nothing, other than the body, of course, but you know that. Nasty business.

INSPECTOR enters.

INSPECTOR
(shows his badge)
Dobrriy den. Inspector Ivonovich, People's Commissariat of Internal Affairs.

NICK
If you like, I can bring you up to speed on the latest developments.

INSPECTOR
I appreciate your enthusiasm, Mr. Charles, but we will take things from here.

NICK
Absolutely!

INSPECTOR
We do things differently here in Russia. We are about facts, not theories.

NICK
The fact is, I have no theories. I am happy to turn this case over to you. I am, in fact, on hiatus.

NORA
Well, he was, Inspector, but I have some crucial shopping to do in the haberdashery department. These lovely people certainly had nothing to do with this, and Nicky is so used to these kinds of cases. Why, he solved the Case of the Corpulent Corpse before the body was even cold. I am sure you...

INSPECTOR
And you are...?

NICK
My wife. Mrs. Charles.

NORA
Charmed, I'm sure.

MME. RANEVSKAYA
(exasperated)
Can we get on with things, please?

INSPECTOR
(clearly smitten)
Ah, MME. Ranevskaya! It has been some time. Welcome back.

MME. RANEVSKAYA
I don't remember our paths crossing. Our family has always been highly respectable. We have had no dealings with police.

INSPECTOR
Of course not. It was a party, years ago. You invited the whole village. The champagne was flowing. You danced the varu varu. You wore red. Most impressive.

MME. RANEVSKAYA
So you remember this house as it was. As it still is in my heart. I would say it had gone to the dogs, but even the dogs are gone.

ANYA
Well, mama, you could hardly expect...

INSPECTOR
Could this be?? Little kotyonok?

ANYA
Anya, and I don't...

INSPECTOR
You wouldn't. You must have been eight or nine. Katarina Stepanova's general store. You had stolen a bauble. A trinket of some kind.

ANYA
That was you?

INSPECTOR
Da.

MME. RANEVSKAYA
Anya?

ANYA
I remember. Mama had lost a brooch, or it was stolen. Mama was beside

ANYA (Cont.)

herself. She always put such value on personal belongings. I thought if I replaced it, mama would smile again.

(to INSPECTOR)

You... You let me keep it if I swept Mme. Stepanova's floor.

INSPECTOR

It was fair trade, lapochka. It was only costume jewelry. You were a terrible criminal. Cried piteously when you were caught.

ANYA

I learned the riches that are in your heart cannot be stolen. I am afraid Mama has yet to learn that lesson.

INSPECTOR

Your loyalty to your mother has always been touching, Miss Anya. It seems like both her daughters would go to any length to protect her.

VARYA

Only from herself. Mama is often too generous with her money, and her love.

NORA

Not everyone is lucky enough to be on a permanent honeymoon like Nicky and me. Right, Nicky?

NICK nods in agreement and takes another drink.

ANYA

Mama looks strong, but she has been through a lot, Inspector. She is not the woman you once knew.

NICK

Neither am I!

NORA

Quiet, Nicky!

NICK
Drink, Inspector?
(pours two)

INSPECTOR
I prefer to be clear-headed, thank you.

NICK
That makes one of us.

He downs both drinks.

INSPECTOR
Is it possible that you ladies tried to reason with Mr. Yepikov? With your
mother's best interests at heart? Maybe things just got out of hand?

MME. RANEVSKAYA
Not possible at all. I raised good girls. And Anya traveled with me from
Paris. We only arrived yesterday.

ANYA
And Varya was engaged to Mr. Yepikov. Well, sort of. It was
complicated.

VARYA
Inspector, you are barking up the wrong tree here.

INSPECTOR
What tree would that be? Looks like Mr. Yepikov had no need for trees
of any kind. I could see that being a rather large bone of contention for
you.

SIMON
This is ridiculous. Varya never knew he was here. We were both in the
dark. I was killing myself trying to prepare for their arrival. He left no
instructions at all.

INSPECTOR
Mr. Smirnov, I presume?

SIMON
We've met. I wore blue.

INSPECTOR
I understand you've had some issues with Mr. Yepikov.

SIMON
Issues? I'll say we had issues. The man was a cad and a swindler. But I
certainly didn't kill him.

INSPECTOR
Do you own any firearms, Mr. Smirnov?

SIMON
Me? Not hardly. Guns give me the willies.

INSPECTOR
It seems Mr. Yepikov was shot with a 38 at close range.

SIMON
I wouldn't even know what a 38 looks like. I don't even shoot pool. I
never raced in school because starter pistols made me wet my pants.

VARYA
I could have lived my whole life without knowing that.

INSPECTOR
Mr. Yepikov - did he own any firearms?

SIMON
How should I know?

There is a pause.

PETER
Actually, he did. A landowner would be foolish not to protect himself in
these dangerous times.
(offers his hand to INSPECTOR, who does not take it)
Peter Trovimov. Pleased to meet you. I have been staying in the guest
cottage, at Mr. Yepikov's behest.

MME. RANEVSKAYA snorts.

MME. RANEVSKAYA
Mr. Yepikov's loyalty seems somewhat displaced. It appears only Peter
has been reaping the benefits of my former home.

INSPECTOR
Did that include access to the firearms, perhaps?

PETER
I am a student of non-violent resistance. It is through my words, not
actions, that I conduct myself.

ANYA
Yes. Lots and lots of words. I can vouch for that!

PETER
I have no idea where things are kept around here.

VARYA
Except the food. You have no trouble finding that.

MME. RANEVSKAYA
Everything that was ours was sold, Inspector, except that bookcase. Too
heavy to move, I suppose. And that desk. It belonged to my father.

SIMON
Wait! I just remembered something.

INSPECTOR
What's that, Mr. Smirnov?

SIMON
Oh, it was years ago. Right after the sale of the house. Mr. Yepikov was worried about retaliation.

VARYA
From whom? We'd all left. Except poor Firs.

ANYA
Poor Firs. Alone and forgotten.

NICK
I think we can safely rule out Firs.

SIMON
It's not like me to speak ill of the dead but... Yepikov continued to make terrible business decisions. He made a lot of enemies along the way.

INSPECTOR
Where are you leading us, Mr. Smirnov?

SIMON
Just that, he did have a gun. He locked it in the desk. When he fled, he said he had betrayed a thieves code by allying with the government, and that they may come looking for him or try to seize the house. Yepikov was always full of hot air, so I gave this no mind. No one ever came by. We had fewer and fewer guests. I never had a need for the gun.

He goes to the desk and jiggles it.

SIMON
Still locked.

INSPECTOR
And where, pray tell, is the key?

SIMON
Must be around here somewhere.

ANYA
Oh, I love a good game of hot and cold.

Starts rummaging around. The others wait a moment and then start helping her. ANYA is going meticulously through the old bookcase, lifting the tacky snow globes and pictures. She is being very thorough, and maybe we should notice she may be looking for something specific. She lifts the picture of Yepikov, sneers at it, and is about to put it down when she hears a sound.

ANYA
Oh, oh!!!

She opens the back of the picture and retrieves a key.

ANYA
Is this it? Did I win?

SIMON
Let me see.

SIMON opens the desk and retrieves a small gun case.

SIMON
Here you go, Inspector.

INSPECTOR opens the box.

INSPECTOR
It's empty.

SIMON
What? That's impossible!

INSPECTOR
(examining the box closely)
Clearly not. Would you have any idea what might have happened to it?

SIMON
No. I haven't touched that desk in years.

NICK
Maybe not. But someone has. May I, Inspector ?

INSPECTOR
(holding the box out to him)
Alright, Mr. Sherlock Holmes. What do you see in this box that I do not?

NICK
Not the box, Inspector. The desk.
(walks over to the desk)
Mr. Smirnov is correct. This desk has not been used in some time. You
see, when I lift this flask, there is a ring of dust around it. Yet there is no
dust around or on top of the case. There is dust on the sides, meaning
someone recently slid it out and carefully put it back.

NORA
Oh Nicky, you are so clever!

NICK
Oh, I am sure Inspector Ivonovich would have noticed this right away.

INSPECTOR
Yes. I would have. You Americans are so quick to spring into action.

NICK
My apologies.

INSPECTOR
Miss Anya, you found that missing key rather quickly.

ANYA

I'm good. I'm really good. Whenever mama lost her reading glasses, I was always the one to find them.

VARYA

Yes, but they were usually on top of her head!

INSPECTOR

Maybe you will have as much luck locating the missing weapon, Miss Anya. You, Mr. Smirnov, as the Americans might say, are in very hot water. You had both motive and opportunity. You had access to a possible murder weapon, and you have shifty eyes. I do not trust what you say. But here in Moscow, we must have hard evidence to convict. I am watching you closely, Mr. Smirnov. Do not try anything funny. In the meantime, I will dust this case for fingerprints.

SIMON

But I handed it to you! Of course my prints are on it!

NICK

You touched the sides of the box. Not the latch or the inside. Right, Inspector?

INSPECTOR

Quite right. Now, I must ask you to please let us handle it from here, Monsieur Hercule Poirot. You will just cause trouble for everyone if you interfere with our investigation.

NICK

Stepping aside, Inspector Ivonovich. I leave things in your capable hands. The only things in my hands from now on will be my drink and Mrs. Charles.

INSPECTOR

I need to make one thing perfectly clear. Though Mr. Smirnov is a particular person of interest, no one here is above suspicion. You may not leave the premises for any reason.

MME. RANEVSKAYA
So we are trapped? For how long?

INSPECTOR
Until this investigation has been settled to my satisfaction. I don't want this gun to suddenly appear in the trash bin of Babaev's chocolate shop in town.

MME. RANEVSKAYA
I would never go there. It's ridiculously overpriced.

VARYA
But what will we do for food, Inspector? We are almost out.

NORA
Don't worry, Nicky will...

NICK interrupts her, putting his arms around her and squeezing.

NICK
Nick will go to the village for provisions. I am happy to have a police escort, Inspector. Will that satisfy you?

INSPECTOR
Yes. That will be sufficient. We will be in touch, Mr. Charles. Mr. Smirnov, do not take the easy way out by using that gun on yourself. This house has seen enough misfortune. I will return shortly. I trust you will all be here. Alive. Once someone gets a taste of murder, it's a hard habit to break. Good day.

INSPECTOR exits through the back. We see him dragging the body from the pool area to offstage. Nobody helps him. Pause. Everyone is looking at SIMON.

SIMON
Why are you all looking at me? I didn't do anything. Nora, you know I couldn't possibly do this.

NORA
Of course you couldn't. Nicky! Do something!

NICK
I think I shall have another drink. Anyone joining me?

MME. RANEVSKAYA
How can you be so cavalier?

NICK
You heard the man. My hands are tied. I suspect this will be like cooking a frog.

SIMON
According to the Inspector, my goose is already cooked.

PETER
All this talk of food is making me hungry. I'm going to see what morsels I can scrape together. Coming, Anya?

ANYA
I'm not hungry.
(PETER gives her a knowing look)
Oh! Yes. Coming.

They exit.

SIMON
MME. Ranevskaya, I swear...

MME. RANEVSKAYA
Don't swear. It's vulgar. I want no more shame heaped on my family. Come, Varya. I am retiring to my room before anyone else is murdered.

VARYA
Oh, honestly, Mama!

VARYA looks at SIMON for a moment, sighs, then exits. We see she still has the letter opener. NORA goes and hugs SIMON and looks at NICK. NICK shrugs his shoulders and goes to get another drink. SIMON exits.

NICK and NORA are alone in the living room. They are drinking. The quiet is palpable. After a moment...

NORA
Oh, Nicky. This is terrible.

NICK
Probably watered down. Here, take mine.
(offers her his drink)

NORA
No. It's Simon. I'm worried for him. You know he didn't do this.

NICK
I know nothing of the kind. I only met the man yesterday.

NORA
Well, I know.

NICK
Your woman's intuition has been wrong before.

NORA
That's what my father told me on our wedding day. I am certainly not wrong now. He's just not capable. He was always such a gentle boy.

NICK
That was a good many years ago, my dear.

NORA
When we were kids, he had this ratty cat. Raskolnikov. He loved that thing. One time, we were playing hide and seek and I heard this

NORA (Cont.)
agonizing scream from the closet. Simon runs out with Raskolnikov in
his arms. I guess the cat must have crawled into the closet to die. Rigor
mortis had set it and it was cold and as stiff as a board, but he wouldn't
put it down. It took a lot if coaxing to put it in one of his mom's travel
bags. We buried it in Central Park.

NICK
This doesn't help your case, dear. Finding poor Firs stuck to the chair
might have sent him over the edge.

NORA
He wouldn't have invited us here if he were planning a murder. He
knows I'm married to the world's greatest detective.

NICK
And most handsome.

NORA
Of course.

NICK
With a debonair charm.

NORA
Just what I was about to say.
(kisses him)
So you'll help him?

NICK
Nope.

NORA
What?

NICK
It's out if my hands, dear. The inspector made that quite clear.

NORA
But Nicky! Police make mistakes all the time!

NICK
And I don't?

NORA
You don't.
(kisses him)

NICK
You are very persuasive, Mrs. Charles.

NORA
I know you, Nicky. You wouldn't let the wrong man go down. It's not in your nature. I want to help. I can search the other cottages and the toolshed. If we could just find that missing gun.

NICK
You need to stay put, my apple blossom. I could use a little more persuading.

NORA
(kisses him again)
How's this?

NICK
You are getting to me like my ninth martini. Keep going.

They continue to kiss as lights dim and cross-fade to ANYA and PETER in the next scene.

TRANSITION WITH MUSIC

SCENE 6

Suggested transition music music: You're An Education - Larry Clinton;
Bea Wain, vocal (1938).

PETER and ANYA sitting on a bench outside.

ANYA
It's freezing out here.

PETER
Here, take my coat.
(drapes his coat over her shoulders)
You look beautiful in the moonlight.

They start to kiss.

ANYA
I don't want to make a fool of myself like last time.

PETER
I was the fool. Life and love are precious things. Let's not waste another
minute.

ANYA
You hurt me. But I never stopped loving you. You were the first boy I
ever kissed.

PETER
And I want to be the last.

He leans over to kiss her. VARYA enters.

VARYA
Dinner's ready!

ANYA
We'll be right in.

VARYA doesn't move.

VARYA
Whatever he's trying to sell you, Anya, don't buy it. He's a fake. He's an emotional cripple. He sponged off Mama for years and now he's sponging off Simon. He's worthless, Anya.

ANYA
You must be freezing, Varya, out here without a coat. Please, let's all go inside. I'm sure Varya's made a wonderful meal.

VARYA
Peter should know. He's eaten enough of them! See if you can restrain yourself from second helpings until everyone's had firsts. Honestly, Anya, you should see him eat! Like an actor! Don't know where he stores it, years of free meals and he's still as scrawny as a tubercular ferret.

VARYA exits.

ANYA
Shall we?

They walk through the doors into the living room / dining area.

TRANSITION WITH MUSIC

SCENE 7

Suggested transition music: I Double Dare You - Larry Clinton; Bea Wain, vocal (1938).

In the dining area. A table is set with the finest place settings they could find. However, they are all mismatched. Everyone is present except SIMON and VARYA.

NICK

Ah! Glad we are all here now. While rummaging through that enormous stack of unopened mail, I found something disturbing that may be of great interest to you.

ANYA

Mail? Please Mr. Charles, Let me see that.

NICK

Looking for something in particular, Miss Anya?

ANYA

No. Of course not. I took handwriting analysis in Paris. And I collect stamps.

NICK

I see. No, everything is local. No stamps for your album, my dear. I have here a letter from lawyers Vasilev and Sokolov. It appears Mr. Yepikov ignored both his correspondence and his fiduciary duties. He has not paid the taxes or the mortgage payments since purchasing Cherry Manor. It is due to go up for auction again on the first.

ANYA

Oh no!

MME. RANEVSKAYA

That's next week!

NICK
Apparently so. The Manor has depreciated somewhat, due to his failure to maintain the property. The auction will start at 30,000 rubles, but is not expected to exceed 70,000.

ANYA
Doesn't matter. Might as well be a million. We haven't got a ruble.

MME. RANEVSKAYA
So now I must suffer the humiliation of losing my home twice. How else will the universe punish me?

SIMON enters from outside.

SIMON
Mr. Charles, The pool has been drained.

VARYA enters with a large bowl of beans.

SIMON
I am afraid this was at the bottom.

Hands over a gun. VARYA screams and drops the bowl of beans.

VARYA
My gun!

NICK
I knew someone would spill the beans!

(OPTIONAL INTERMISSION HERE)

VARYA
(to SIMON)
You said you'd get rid of it!

SIMON
How was I supposed to know it was yours? You told me to look in your mother's room!

MME. RANEVSKAYA
My room? How dare you? Varya, how could you?

VARYA
I was just trying to protect you, Mama. I didn't do this! Nora, you believe me, don't you? I couldn't possibly...

NORA
Of course you couldn't. Of course she didn't, Nicky.

NICK
(examining the gun)
This is a 22. Mr. Yepikov was shot with a 38.

NORA
You see, dear? That's a 16-point difference!

NICK
So, now we have two guns and no murder weapon. This family is getting more interesting by the minute. But this doesn't explain how your gun happened to wind up at the bottom of the pool.

NORA
Yes, dear, just tell us.

VARYA
I have no idea. Really, I don't.

PETER steps forward.

PETER
I am afraid I am to blame, Mr. Charles.

VARYA
You?

PETER
Forgive me, Varya. I saw the gun in your purse when you first arrived here. I didn't think much of it at the time... but after Mr. Yepikov was shot, I just assumed...
(to NICK)
I mean, it's no secret he was a scoundrel to her... I took the gun and just tossed it. It didn't occur to me at the time that the pool would get drained. I was horrified when Mr. Charles suggested it. Believe it or not, I did it to protect you, Varya, because... Well, I love Anya. There, I said it; and Anya loves you, Varya. I know there is no love lost between us and I was desperate to change your opinion of me. I figured if there was no murder weapon, maybe the intruder theory would fly, and we could all just get on with our lives. When Simon found the gun, I really should have said something, but I had wiped off any fingerprints and thought surely Varya wouldn't claim it was hers!! I know it was wrong, all of it...

NICK is exasperated.

MME. RANEVSKAYA
You are a bumbling idiot. You are stupider than I gave you credit for.

PETER
I am so sorry. Varya, can you ever forgive me?

VARYA
I'm at a loss for words.

NICK
I see chivalry is not only dead, it's decomposing!

ANYA
You did this for me? Oh Peter, you stupid fool. I would have told you Varya is not capable of such a violent act. She faints at the sight of an underdone steak.

MME. RANEVSKAYA
Really. This is most absurd. I raised both my daughters better than that!

PETER
Yes, of course. But Varya's adopted. There is no telling what evil might be lurking in her bloodline. And crimes of passion are predominately done by women, isn't that right, Mr. Charles?

The women are appalled at this suggestion.

NICK
Statistically speaking, yes, but we have yet to determine the motive. All we know is that he was shot in the back, and dumped in the pool after he was dead. Crimes of passion tend to be a little more spontaneous. That being said, when did you adopt Varya, MME. Ranevskaya? What do you know about her parentage?

MME. RANEVSKAYA
Peter is an imbecile! He lived in this house with Varya for years! I adopted her when she was nine years old. She had lost both her parents.

NICK
I can understand losing one, but both? Now that just seems careless.

MME. RANEVSKAYA
You are trying my patience, Mr. Charles!

NICK
Don't mind if I do. And if you are ever in New York, you must come by and try ours.

SIMON
Really, can't we just sit down and eat? The soup's getting cold.

VARYA
It's Vichyssoise. It's supposed to be cold.

NICK
Simon's right. Let's eat. I'm thirsty.

They move to sit down. NICK holds out a chair for MME.
RANEVSKAYA. She bristles.

MME. RANEVSKAYA
I certainly don't want to sit next to you! It will activate my dyspepsia.

NICK moves aside. PETER is now next to her.

MME. RANEVSKAYA
You either, you mental defective!
(pushes him aside)

NICK
I wasn't aware we were in for a round of musical chairs.

NICK begins whistling loudly and walking around the chairs.

NORA
Nicky, be still. Come here and sit by me.

NICK
Mrs. Charles, you drive me to drink. And for that, I am eternally grateful.

One side of the table has ANYA, MME. RANEVSKAYA and VARYA.
PETER and SIMON are at either end with NICK and NORA on the
opposite side. They eat in silence for a moment. We hear the clinking of
spoons. NICK is drinking. They are all looking at each other
suspiciously. Suddenly, VARYA throws down her spoon.

VARYA
I can't stand it. I just can't stand it.

She throws down her napkin and runs off.

ANYA
Varya!

She gets up and follows her. PETER follows ANYA. MME.
RANEVSKAYA is left looking at SIMON and NICK.

MME. RANEVSKAYA
I've just lost my appetite. Simon, Draw me a bath. I am retiring!

She gets up and leaves in a huff. SIMON clears the plates and goes
upstairs. NICK and NORA are left alone at the table.

NICK
Ahhh! Alone at last, Mrs. Charles!

NORA
Bon appetit, Mr. Charles!

They clink their glasses and enjoy their meal as lights fade.

LIGHTS FADE TO 25%, MUSIC PLAYS

SCENE 8

Suggested transition music: Let A Little Pleasure Interfere With Business - Dave Frost & his Cafe De Paris Band (1931).

MONTAGE:

NICK and NORA repeatedly pour themselves drinks. NICK gets up and dances around in time to the music. SIMON passes through, dances a turn with NICK, cleans up the dinner plates from the table and exits. NICK becomes more unstable, makes his way over to a bench or couch, lies down, puts a napkin over his face and passes out. NORA is slumped across the table.

MUSIC CROSSFADES TO BIRD SOUNDS. LIGHTS FADE UP.

The next morning. Sunlight is streaming through the windows. Birds are chirping. The coffee is in the samovar. NORA wakes up slowly, cautiously, nursing a huge headache. She groans.

NORA
Oh, Nicky! Those birds! Can't you quiet them down?

NICK
(shushes them, then slowly sits up and pulls the napkin off his face)
Persistent little devils, aren't they?

NORA
The room is still spinning.

NICK
No one asked you to drink everything on the table last night.

He crosses to her uneasily, wraps some ice in a hand towel and puts it on her head.

BIRDS FADE 50%

75

NORA
The bottle was open. It would have gone flat otherwise.

NICK
Yes, nothing worse than flat vodka. Coffee, my dear?

NICK pours himself a cup, then pulls out a bottle from the cabinet or shelf, and adds a drop of whiskey to his coffee. He sighs with delight and sits down.

NORA
Ummmmm...
(she kisses him)
You taste familiar.

NICK
Perhaps you'd like a little hair of the dog?

NORA grimaces.

NORA
Oh!! I miss Asta! Just coffee, please.

NICK prepares a cup for her. She drinks and feels a bit of life restoring.

NORA
I'm sorry, dear. This has been a dreadful vacation. It's cold, my bed is lumpy, I don't like borscht, I never got my new hat, and now we're out of scotch!

BIRDS FADE OUT

NICK
Not to mention there is a murderer among us.

NORA
Oh, that. You'll solve it. You're a great detective.

NICK

A really good detective never gets married.

NORA

They can't all be as lucky as you, dear. Anyway, no further detecting after this. I need you all to myself.

MME. RANEVSKAYA enters.

MME. RANEVSKAYA

I'm afraid we all need you, Mr. Charles, as insufferable as you are. The Ranevskayas still have a decent reputation in these parts. I'd like to avoid any unnecessary police activity and keep this a family affair, if possible. I appreciate your efforts, though I can't say I'll be sorry to see the back of you.

NICK

Some say that's my best feature. With your permission, I shall proceed.

NORA

Coffee, MME. Ranevskaya? It's fresh.

MME. RANEVSKAYA

Yes, please.

She does not move. NORA pours her a cup while carefully balancing the towel filled with ice on her head

MME. RANEVSKAYA

Where is Simon?

NORA

I heard him puttering around in the kitchen. Perhaps he's getting the breakfast ready.

MME. RANEVSKAYA

Good. ...Mr. Charles, it's not like me to cast aspersions–

NICK
Of course not. Cast away.

MME. RANEVSKAYA
I think the inspector is right. If anyone had a reason to kill Mr. Yepikov, it was Simon.

NICK
How so?

NORA
I don't believe that for a second.

MME. RANEVSKAYA
Dear Nora, you have not seen Simon for a great many years. Do not be so bold as to presume you know him. Simon has been a virtual prisoner here.

NICK
He chose to stay here, did he not?

MME. RANEVSKAYA
What choice did he have? Yepikov abandoned him, as he abandoned my poor Varya. He left Simon with no salary, no money for upkeep, and, as you can see, my home has been reduced to rubble. Goodness knows what its done to his mind. Oh, you should have seen this place in its glory. Carpets from Scandinavia, lace drapes from Belgium. Not a speck of dust. Simon remembers. Simon might have married, been happy. Yepikov robbed him of years of his life.

SIMON and VARYA enter with breakfast things.

SIMON
We are lucky to have Varya here. She made potato rolls from scratch. For the record, I was not a prisoner, Mr. Charles. I stayed out of loyalty.

MME. RANEVSKAYA
To whom?

SIMON
To you! And Varya and Anya. This home, by all rights, should belong to
you. Yepikov never cared one scintilla about your home. He just bought
it because he could. I always thought it was out of spite, and now we
know. He let everything lapse, and now the house will be sold again. It is
you who were robbed, MME. Ranevskaya, not I.

ANYA and PETER enter from outside.

MME. RANEVSKAYA
And where have you been, young lady?

ANYA
Just walking, Mama. Morning, Varya.

VARYA
Morning.
(looks at them both with raised eyebrows, knowingly)

PETER
Is that fresh bread?
(grabs some)
Oh, delectable! Funny how everything tastes better all of a sudden. And
the coffee! The power of a man's mind is in direct proportion to the
quality and quantity of his morning coffee. All those years, I never gave
it much thought. The servants made the coffee. Then, when I was on my
own, I realized I didn't even know the ingredients for a good cup. This is
the nectar of the angels.

VARYA
It's the same coffee we've always had, but Simon added some cinnamon.

SIMON
It was Varya's idea.

ANYA
Save some for Mama. You know she needs three or four cups before she feels like herself.

NORA
And I need another cup to NOT feel like myself.

SIMON
Rough night?

NORA
You might say that.

PETER
(to ANYA)
Actually, my love, I am in need of a good long soak. May I avail myself of your facilities?

MME. RANEVSKAYA
Too lazy to walk across to your cottage?

PETER
My tub is not working at all. I think the pipes must be frozen. It's positively Dickensian out there. I have been writing with gloves on.

VARYA
I wonder what else you have been doing to keep warm.

ANYA
Go ahead. There are lavender epsom salts on the shelf. Very soothing.

PETER
(whispering to ANYA)
Care to join me?

ANYA blushes.

MME. RANEVSKAYA
That is highly improper, young man!

PETER
(kisses MME. RANEVSKAYA'S hand)
Not for much longer, I hope. See you in a bit.

Runs upstairs. There is a pause. MME. RANEVSKAYA and VARYA are looking at ANYA. It is uncomfortable.

MME. RANEVSKAYA
Well, you two have certainly gotten cozy in a hurry.

ANYA
I never knew him to be like this. He appears to have undergone some deep emotional metamorphosis. So excited about life. So enthusiastic about the future.., our future. Oh, it may be reckless of me to fall so hard, so quickly, but Peter's not exactly a stranger.

VARYA
This Peter certainly is.

SIMON
Yes. I would urge you to err on the side of caution. Two weeks ago, his nose was in a book and I couldn't get three words out of him. You could hear him typing into the wee hours, but all I ever saw was piles of crumpled paper. He slept until the afternoon and only came inside to eat. This metamorphosis of his is rather suspect. Do you suppose he might have gotten a hold of some of your medication, Varya?

VARYA
Simon!

SIMON
Oh, there I go again.

MME. RANEVSKAYA

No. There will be no secrets here anymore. Varya has been suffering from a nervous condition, Mr. Charles. Brought about by stress no doubt. When I was forced to go back to Paris, Varya got a job working as a housekeeper for some dreadful children. Cordon Blue trained, and all those brats ever wanted was baked beans on toast! And they would torture her, putting snakes and lizards in her bed at night, stashing all her undergarments in the ice box. She was a basket case by the time she finally left. Under a doctor's care. But she's much better now, aren't you, dear?

VARYA

Some days I think so, but I just don't know. Other days are still foggy. The other night I woke up and found myself in the kitchen eating raspberry Vatrushka buns and making a tiramisu. I have no idea how I got there.

NICK

Would you mind if I had a look at your medication?

VARYA

Not at all. I keep it in the upstairs bathroom. Oh, it's occupied right now.

ANYA

I'll get it.

MME. RANEVSKAYA

You'll do nothing of the kind, young lady. I am sure we can all wait until we are all present and accounted for.

NICK

Yes. Not to worry. If we could all just sit down for a bit, I'd like to ask a few questions.

ANYA

I, for one, have nothing to hide.

NICK

There's a skeleton in every closet. If you rattle it long enough, something's bound to come out. So, Anya, how did you feel about Mr. Yepikov?

ANYA

He was older. More Mama's friend than ours. I couldn't really see why Varya was so interested in him. Rather dull, if you ask me.

NICK

And how did you feel when he didn't come through for your sister?

ANYA

I had no feelings about it, one way or the other.

NICK

Now, for me to really help here, I need the truth. Undiluted, like my scotch. If Yepikov had married Varya like everyone thought, this house would have stayed in the family, would it not?

ANYA

It would have, but Varya would have been miserable. I know she thought he was her best chance but....

NICK

But you knew differently, didn't you, Anya?

ANYA

Alright! He was a ghastly, vulgar little man. Varya, I never told you this, but, well... he promised me things too. He made his intentions quite clear one night, and I slapped his stupid face. He laughed and called all the Ranevskayas pathetic. That we were... forgive me, Mama– only good for one thing, just like our mama. He said he knew this from experience. What did he mean, Mama?

MME. RANEVSKAYA

That loathsome, hateful swine! How dare he?

VARYA
Oh, Mama, you didn't!

MME. RANEVSKAYA
God forgive me. This was something I vowed never to tell.

ANYA
Mama, don't. Some things are better left unsaid.

MME. RANEVSKAYA
No, I must clear the air once and for all.

NICK
Go on, Mme. Ranevskaya. You are among friends.

MME. RANEVSKAYA
We were mere children. I couldn't have been more than 15. Gregor
Yepikov's father worked for us. The man was a barbarian. Beat poor
Gregor mercilessly. Once, Gregor came to the house to make a delivery.
His nose was bleeding and he didn't even have a handkerchief. I was
alone. Papa was out in the fields and Mama was in the village. I took him
into the kitchen and I cleaned his face. I looked at his neck and saw other
marks. Deep cuts, maybe from a belt. I started to clean those as well. I
had to remove his shirt to treat the wounds. I had never seen a man's
body before... except Papa's, the time I had to bring more hot water into
the bath, but I looked away then. I could not take my eyes off his skin.
Hairless. Beautiful. Before I knew it, he was kissing me, and I didn't stop
him... He lifted me onto the kitchen table. His hands reached for my... It
was my first time. After it was over, he put back on his shirt and told me
I had to pay for the grocery delivery. I went into Mama's money box,
paid him and gave him a fifty-ruble tip! The next time I saw him, it was
as if nothing had ever happened. He never mentioned it again, and
neither did I. By the time you two began your flirtation, he was getting
rich and I thought he would take care of you. The past was the past and it
didn't matter.

ANYA

The kitchen table? The one we all ate breakfast at? Oh, I shall never be able to look at it again.

VARYA

That repulsive, sickening beast. You should have told me, Mama, I never would have... Oh, how I hate him. And Anya... if you told me, I would have killed him right then!

NICK

Instead of later?

VARYA

Oh, don't be ridiculous. I already told you I didn't kill him. Though it would have saved me a lot of heartache if I had. I only flirted with him because, well, there was no one else. Have you been to the village, Mr. Charles? Very slim pickings. Gregor was old, but he had money. Mama had lost everything and I thought, well, it's him or the convent. I don't look good in black and I like lipstick and perfume. Not that he paid much attention. I know I'm not as clever or pretty as Anya, but I've been told I'm not too hard on the eyes.

NORA

You're absolutely lovely, dear.

VARYA

Gregor was no beauty contest winner, that's for sure, but I would have made it work. I thought being his wife would have been advantageous.

NICK

For who?

VARYA

For Mama. I wanted her to know she could always come home again. I waited for him to realize a union would be beneficial for us both. I got nothing. I stayed in that abysmal job, being driven mad by those mean-spirited children, and I lost myself. When Simon told me he called us

85

VARYA (Cont.)
back here for the holidays, I thought there was hope. But if I knew then what I know now...

SIMON
The man is... was, an idiot. Then and now. I had no idea he had... made the rounds among the Ranevskayas. If I had thought I had a chance with you back then, I never would have let you leave.

VARYA
Simon? I didn't have a clue.

SIMON
You wanted truth, Mr. Charles? There's your truth. I have loved Varya as long as I have known her. She is a beautiful, spirited woman who speaks her mind, and Yepikov didn't deserve her. If he had wanted her back, I don't know what I would have done. I didn't kill him, but I know I wished him gone. Now that he is, I will do everything in my power to show Varya that I am more than the mealy-mouthed caretaker who kowtowed to everyone. I will show her I am a real man, worthy of her love.

VARYA
What a surprising morning this is turning out to be!

PETER enters freshly showered and dressed.

PETER
Well, love is certainly in the air today. Nothing like a fatal shooting to bring one's feelings bubbling to the surface.

ANYA
Feeling refreshed?

PETER
Remarkably so. I always felt Simon harbored untold passions. How brave of you to unearth it now, when you have no competition.

86

ANYA

I think it's wonderful.

NORA

Me, too. Good for you, Simon.
(gives him a hug)
The right woman is worth waiting for. Isn't that right, Nicky?

NICK

I don't know. I am still waiting. You are good for right now, I suppose.

NORA

I keep a list of possible replacements somewhere. Oh, here it is.

NORA kicks him in the shin.

NICK

I stand corrected. I am the luckiest man alive.
(kisses her)

VARYA
(to PETER)
What about you? Your cup seems to have runneth over as well. You are brimming with happiness, all of a sudden.

PETER

The re-appearance of Anya has moved me profoundly.

NORA

A beautiful face can do that.

NICK

Yes. Look at me. I'm positively ecstatic. Varya, dear, would you be so kind as to run up and get your...

VARYA

Oh, of course, Mr. Charles.

VARYA exits.

NICK
Let's all make ourselves comfortable.
(pours himself another drink)

MME. RANEVSKAYA
Isn't it a bit early for that, Mr. Charles?

NICK
Why? I'm awake. Everyone has been delightfully forthcoming this morning. Peter, would you mind answering a few questions, as well?

PETER
Not at all, Mr. Charles. In fact, it's an honor to be questioned by the great Nick Charles. I followed the Thin Man case meticulously.

NICK
Flattery will get you everywhere. Just ask Mrs. Charles.

NORA
It's true.

NICK
Just how did you come to be in the guest cottage?

PETER
Unlike all of you, apparently, Yepikov was decent to me. He understood my quest for knowledge and the need to better myself. People get stuck here, Mr. Charles, so I went away to finish my studies. Yepikov offered to help, and at first I was too proud or arrogant to accept. But we were communicating, and every so often a small check would arrive. Not much, just enough to keep me in typewriter ribbons and potatoes. As this term was drawing to a close, I needed somewhere quiet to work on my project. "A Critical Approach to Capitalism, Revolution, and Metaphor in Russian Avant-Garde Literary Imagination."

NICK
I believe I saw the film.

PETER
Yepikov offered the cottage to me for as long as I needed it. It wound up being longer than I expected. I know Simon resented my presence, so I tried to stay out of his way. I admit to sinking into a melancholy funk. In fact, it was paralyzing. I tried to focus on other things, but it was hopeless. I hated my writing. All of it. I even thought of taking my own life.

NICK
You seem pretty lively now. What caused the shift? MME. Ranevskaya harbored a pretty bitter grudge.

PETER
Sure, I was nervous when Yepikov wrote and told me he had invited the family back for the holidays. I wasn't sure if that meant I had to leave, or whether this was a chance for me to mend some broken bridges. I know Varya was less than pleased to have me about, but as soon as I saw Anya, I knew. It was as if 20,000 volts of electricity suddenly ripped through me. I was the Frankenstein monster come to life.

VARYA enters.

VARYA
Here's my medication.

She hands it to NICK. NICK shakes it.

NICK
A Benzedrine inhaler. Nearly empty. When was the last time you remember using it?

VARYA
After dinner last night, but before that, it's hard to remember. Not every day, I don't think.

NICK

Benzedrine inhalers were very common with soldiers to combat fatigue.
It's a class A amphetamine. A definite mood enhancer. Sometimes the
inhaler can be opened up like this.
(cracks it open)
See these tiny strips of paper? They are covered in Benzedrine. One can
roll them into tiny balls and take them with their morning coffee.

MME. RANEVSKAYA

What are you insinuating?
(slams down her cup)
Taste it yourself, Mr. Charles. Although if it doesn't taste like alcohol,
you might not know the difference.

NICK

(smells her coffee and hands it back)
Heavenly coffee, despite the lack of enhancements. I would have
detected a slight smell of detergent.

Everyone smells their coffee.

NICK

The inhalers are also good for productivity. Benzedrine causes euphoria,
increased interest in carnal pleasures, and if overused, irrational behavior
and psychosis.

PETER

I haven't touched that thing. I've never seen it before. The only drug I
needed was Anya. She is my muse, the fire in my belly.

VARYA

And elsewhere, apparently.

SIMON

I have been watching Varya closely. I haven't noticed any changes in her
behavior. She has been consistent this whole visit, even with all the

SIMON (Cont.)
upheaval. My bedroom is right by the kitchen. I would have noticed if anyone was wandering about.

ANYA
That first night, Varya never left her room. I know because I heard her pacing around.

VARYA
I was nervous. I wasn't sure what to expect, seeing Gregor after all this time.

NICK
You must not have gotten much sleep yourself, then.

ANYA
It was a long trip. It's hard to wind down. I was nervous too. Peter, and being back here and all. It's all very emotional. I loved this house.

MME. RANEVSKAYA
We all did. Before it went to rack and ruin. This is desecration.

SIMON
I think we could restore it again. If...

MME. RANEVSKAYA
If, if, if... We could have ham and eggs if we had some eggs. Or ham! The Ranevskayas are penniless. Damn my generosity. What has it ever gotten me? Abused, abandoned and forgotten. What is to become of us?

SIMON
Varya has a good eye...

NORA
Two of them, in fact.

SIMON
And she's the most amazing cook. I think together we could...

VARYA
Together?

SIMON
Yes. Together. We can take it slow. At your pace. We don't have to rush
into anything.

VARYA
(throws her arms around him and kisses him)
I'm in!! All in!!

PETER
Such a touching display of affection. Seriously though, I'm delighted for
you both. Just watch out for Varya. She has a mean right hook.

VARYA
Care for a demonstration?

*She goes to punch PETER. SIMON pulls her back, calms her and they
kiss.*

SIMON
I like a woman with spunk. My plucky, spunky, gutsy...

VARYA
Shut up and kiss me.

NORA
Nicky, may I speak to you for a moment? Over here?

NICK
Certainly, my cherry blossom.

NICK and NORA cross the room and whisper together. In the meantime, everyone else is rather celebratory about the coupling of SIMON and VARYA. Patting backs, shaking hands and whatnot.

NICK
Sounds like a capital idea.
(they return to the group)
My little dove has come up with quite an appealing solution. Would you like to do the honors, dear?

NORA
I have to admit, when I first arrived, this place reminded me of Du Maurier's Manderlay, after the fire. So dusty, and gloomy, and filled with meaningless trinkets. It's not your fault, Simon, it needed a woman's touch. More than a touch, it needed to be... loved again. So I've decided... I'm going to buy Cherry Manor!

Everyone ad libs "What? You? That's absurd..." etc.

NORA (cont.)
Yes. And I'm giving it to you, Simon... and Varya... as a wedding gift, I hope. However, I'll have to rethink things if one of you turns out to be the murderer. It's not right to profit from a crime, is it, Nicky?

NICK
Right again, angel. See what you catch being in close proximity to me?

MME. RANEVSKAYA
I'm sure that's not all she catches!

NICK
You run along and start the ball rolling, my love. Worst case scenario, we'll give the house to your mother. That should be a healthy enough distance, don't you think?

NORA
Does this mean you've solved the case? Oh, you are a clever, clever man!

NICK

I always say if you let someone talk long enough, they'll make a slip. There's been quite a lot of tap dancing around here tonight, but I think the show is over. If you'll excuse me for a moment, I'm going to watch my wife divest herself of my monthly drinking rations.

NICK and NORA exit. The rest of them look at each other suspiciously as lights slowly fade to black.

BLACKOUT

SCENE 9

Suggested transition music: True Confession - Larry Clinton; Bea Wain, vocal (1938)

Moments later. Lights up and the group is in the exact positions as they were before. NICK enters. He is holding NORA'S pocketbook and a drink.

SIMON
Well?

NICK
Oh, Nora's left me holding the bag again.

ANYA
Mr. Charles – what happened?

NICK
Negotiations have begun. Nora offered 50,000 rubles and everyone seemed quite pleased with that. No one else has even put in a bid.

MME. RANEVSKAYA
But, what about us? We're all just sitting ducks here.

NICK
Better than Peking ducks. No peeking, anyone!

SIMON
You implied you knew something. Could you just get on with it, please?

NICK
Yes. Do sit down everyone. Make yourselves comfortable.

ANYA
I think this is as comfortable as anyone's going to get!

NICK
I'm afraid I need to ask a few more questions.

ANYA
Fire away...

Everyone groans at this pun again!

ANYA
Sorry... Sorry!

NICK
(refreshing his drink)
MME. Ranevskaya, I hate to bring up a touchy subject...

MME. RANEVSKAYA
Why stop now?

NICK
I know your little boy, Grisha... had a tragic accident.

MME. RANEVSKAYA
Grisha! Oh, my Grisha... Don't you speak his name. He was an angel. A beam of sunlight.

NICK
He drowned, as I recall.

MME. RANEVSKAYA
Yes. He was only seven. Peter was his tutor. I thought he was watching him.

ANYA
Oh, Mama. It was an awful, awful thing. But Peter's not to blame. We were all here eating dinner, remember? He refused to eat his vegetables and you sent him to his room. He must have walked down to the river.

ANYA (Cont.)
He loved catching frogs. He must have slipped on the rocks. When it was
time for his bath, we looked for him frantically. Mama was hysterical.
Peter was in a panic, too.

PETER
I loved that boy.

VARYA
You loved your job, and the free room and board.

PETER
See, what I told you, Simon? Bam! Right hook to the solar plexis.

NICK
Who found him?

ANYA
It was Firs, our servant. He found him and carried him back to the house.
It was clear he was gone. He was blue and his body was as cold as ice.
Mama fainted dead away at the sight.

MME. RANEVSKAYA
My husband... and then my little boy, only a month later. It was so quiet
without them. I couldn't face it. Do you have children, Mr. Charles?

NICK
That particular blessing has been denied us so far. Our children have
been of the canine variety. But I know how you feel, believe me. It must
have been particularly jolting to see that Mr. Yepikov put a pool in the
backyard.

MME. RANEVSKAYA
It was a cold and heartless thing to do.

NICK
You must have been very angry.

MME. RANEVSKAYA
I was furious! But I wouldn't put anything past that snake. He probably built it just to torture me!

ANYA
Mama, I think you should stop talking now.

VARYA
Yes. None of us knew anything about the pool until we got here.

NICK
You arrived first, didn't you?

VARYA
I was closest. I was devastated to see the state of things. I knew Mama would be crushed. Simon and I tried to do what we could, but...

NICK
You couldn't fix this, could you?

VARYA
There wasn't much time. All I wanted was to see Mama happy to be home again. It had been such a long time.

NICK
Yes. She didn't take you with her when she left, did she? She only took Anya.

VARYA
Mama expected Gregor to propose. We all did. That's the only reason I didn't go to Paris. Love makes one suffer so. Why didn't you tell me, Mama? About Gregor? They say time is a great healer. Well, hate is a greater one. I wouldn't have given him another thought if I had known the truth.

MME. RANEVSKAYA
I did what I thought was best for you at the time. Anya was still a child.

MME. RANEVSKAYA (Cont.)
She needed to finish school, find herself.

NICK
Did you, Anya? Find yourself? It seems MME. Ranevskaya was rather
preoccupied with her new man in Paris. I don't expect she had much time
to check up on you. You could have easily gone back to Moscow, met up
with Mr. Yepikov... in secret.

ANYA
We communicated. But it wasn't what you thought. He did ask me to
come, but I refused. I wrote him and told him to stay away from my
family, and me. When he invited us all back for the holidays, I was
afraid. He said he kept all my letters.

NICK
Ah... Those letters...You did seem to have a peculiar fascination with Mr.
Yepikov's private correspondence.

ANYA
I thought he was going to blackmail me, but he said he had a change of
heart. I like to believe the good in all people, Mr. Charles, so I didn't say
anything. I wanted to believe this family could be made whole again.

NICK
It appears you are very good at keeping secrets, Anya.

ANYA
You're right, Mr. Charles. I like to think I am the glue that held this
family together, even if it was based on lies. I preserved the sanctity of
our memories. Of this house. Of our lives. Sometimes, memories are all
you have to keep you moving forward. I didn't like who I had become in
Paris. I was hardened, bitter. Yes, I found myself. I also found Jacques,
Antoine, and Pierre. All in a hopeless attempt to forget Peter's rejection,
and Gregor's vulgar propositions.

NICK
What did you expect to find when you got here?

ANYA
I was overjoyed to see Varya, of course. I stayed up late that night, hoping to catch Mr. Yepikov before the rest of the family. I just wanted to clear the air, to make sure he was on the up and up. I was so nervous. Varya wasn't sleeping either, and I was running all these scenarios in my head. How would I approach him? What would I say? Would he give my letters back? But he never showed up. I was wondering if this all wasn't going to be some cruel trick. I couldn't let that happen.

SIMON
The plot thickens.

NICK
And what about you, Simon? Your smouldering resentment is no secret.

SIMON
I have had no contact with Yepikov at all, not when we were low on supplies, not when the last of the tenants left, not when I was stranded here for months, selling off furniture to keep the gas and lights on. A month ago, Peter showed up with a letter from Yepikov, saying he may occupy a guest cottage for as long as he needs.

NICK
That must have been exceedingly inconvenient.

SIMON
You don't know the half of it. Then I find he's been sending checks to Peter. Another indignity heaped on me. A real slap in the face. I had been eating nothing but cabbage soup and potatoes for weeks! You'd think Peter would contribute a little, but NO! Peter was waltzing around here like he owned the place. I wrote to Yepikov. I told him if I wanted company, I would get a cat. Nothing. I invited you and your Mrs. over here in good faith, because I am very fond of Nora, but I was hoping she might be able to finance a couple trips to the market.

SIMON (Cont.)
Things were looking pretty grim.

NORA
Oh, Simon. You poor thing. If only I had known.

SIMON
I was humiliated enough. Then... Then I get a telegram from Yepikov,
telling me to prepare the house for guests. How was I supposed to do
that? Luckily, Varya came early and we went to the market. She had her
wages from her last job. It's a miracle what she managed to whip together
on a budget.

NICK
Yes, it was quite the epicurean experience.

VARYA
Thank you.

SIMON
I was eager for Mr. Yepikov to arrive, only because I wanted to give him
a piece of my mind. If he didn't do the right thing with Cherry Manor, I
was done. And if he didn't do the right thing with Varya, I was hoping he
would step aside, give me a shot.

VARYA
Poor choice of words, dearest.

NICK
It looks like every single one of you had a good reason to do away with
Mr. Yepikov.

PETER
Not all of us.

NICK
That's right, Peter. You had no earthly reason to harm Mr. Yepikov,

NICK (Cont.)
which makes me wonder why, in fact, you did.

PETER
I didn't kill him.

NICK
I'm afraid you did, Peter. You did your best to frame Varya by stealing her gun and throwing it in the pool, where you were sure it would be found.

PETER
I explained that.

NICK
So you did. Which is why you gave yourself away when you went upstairs to take a bath. If you stayed dirty a few more days, I might not have put it together. You said the pipes were frozen, but I didn't notice you using any of our bathrooms for any other purpose. It was Mrs. Charles who suggested we search the cottages again.

NORA
Thank you, Nicky. I love helping. He rarely lets me, because sometimes I get arrested.

NICK
When I returned to your cottage just now, I found the sink and toilet were working. But you were right. Peter, the tub was not. So I did a little investigating and found out why. It appears this was wedged in the drainage pipe.

NICK pulls a 38 revolver from NORA'S purse. Immediately, PETER pulls out ANYA'S gun and puts it to her head!

ANYA
My gun! Peter, what are you doing?

102

PETER
Very nice of you to give this to me the other day, darling. And it's
loaded, too. One bullet for everyone. Drop the gun, Mr. Charles.

He does.

PETER (cont.)
You are a pretty good detective, after all. Here's what you don't know.
My life was at a standstill. I had become paralyzed, dispassionate, unable
to produce any work worth a damn. I thought of taking my own life. But
then I thought – No! It's not death I crave! It's the fear of never truly
living! I sat and ruminated on this for days. I became obsessed with the
idea of taking a life, any life. It didn't matter. Yepikov came by a couple
days ago. I have no idea what his motives were concerning you people,
and I didn't care. I was bored out of my skull. I brought him into my
cottage and asked him if he would unclog the bathroom drain. As he
stood there, I pulled out my gun – and Bam! I wrapped him in the shower
curtain for a few hours 'til he was good and stiff, and then when everyone
was asleep, I dumped him in the pool. Biologically, we are a very minor
species, not much better than the toads, but after I extinguished his light,
I was filled with an energy and power I never knew existed. I wasn't
merely playing God. I WAS God! Anya... You never looked so
ravishing. So, this is how it's gonna play. You're going to let me leave
here with Anya. If you call the police and they come after me, she gets it.
It's that simple. Or, I could shoot my way out and a lot of people would
get hurt. You all hated Yepikov. There's not a one of you that's sorry he's
dead. Simon, you got a house and the girl out of the deal. Well done!

PETER starts edging towards the kitchen door. ANYA remains terrified.

PETER
So, we'll be leaving you now...

*NORA enters quietly behind them with a champagne bottle. She assesses
the situation and hits PETER on the head breaking the bottle. PETER
falls to the floor and ANYA runs to VARYA and SIMON. NICK quickly
approaches PETER, kicks his gun away and looks for something to tie*

him up with. Finding nothing, MME. RANEVSKAYA offers her sash or if anyone is wearing a tie, they whip that off and hand it to NICK. He ties up PETER.

NORA
I'm sorry, Nicky! What a waste of a perfectly good bottle of champagne.*

NICK
Call Inspector Ivonovich. Tell him his Christmas present just arrived early.

BLACKOUT

~~~~~~

*NOTE:
In the original production, we found breakable bottles difficult to handle, so we had NORA use a cookie sheet, which made a nice, satisfying bang. We changed her line, as well. Feel free to use this as an alternate ending.

NORA
Oh Nicky! I think my kitchen skills are finally improving!

SCENE 10

*Suggested transition music: It Looks Like Rain In Cherry Blossom Lane -
Guy Lombardo; Lebert Lombardo, vocal (1937).*

*A few minutes later. PETER is well tied up and in a chair. NORA is
putting a towel full of ice on his head wound.*

MME. RANEVSKAYA
Don't pamper him, Nora. He deserves to be in pain. I never did trust you,
you disgusting animal.

NORA
It's just to keep him conscious 'til Inspector Ivonovich arrives. Believe
me, MME. Ranevskaya, he'll have plenty of pain in the Gulag, or
wherever they send him.

PETER
I'll fight this and I'll win. I'm smarter than any Slavic lawyer. Even if
they kill me, I'll win. My work will be published posthumously and I'll
be rich and famous like Van Gogh.

ANYA
Oh... Your book? I might have "accidentally" put it in the fireplace. I was
getting a little chilly with that cold gun against my temple. Don't know
what I was thinking! I must have been temporarily insane. But you'll
have time to write it again... Genius that you are.

PETER
Anya, how could you? My love for you was real, as real as your beloved
cherry orchard.

VARYA
You disgusting, lying cheat! You ruined our lives! I should kill you right
now!

VARYA whips out the letter opener and runs to PETER to stab him.

ANYA
Varya! No!! He's not worth it!

NORA
Let me take that, dear.

Calmly takes the letter opener from VARYA. VARYA appears to calm down but then rushes towards PETER again.

VARYA
This is for your cherry orchard!

She kicks him in the balls, PETER groans. The doorbell rings.

NICK
Ah! That will be Inspector Ivonovich. I think Peter's cherry orchard will be a five by seven cell for the foreseeable future.

NICK goes to the door. INSPECTOR IVONOVICH enters.

INSPECTOR
I appreciate your call, Mr. Charles. But it was completely unnecessary. Mr. Trovimov's fingerprints were all over the gun case.

INSPECTOR looks at NORA who is still clutching the large letter opener in her hand.

NORA
Oh, darn these hangnails.
(begins to file her nails with the letter opener)
Can we get you anything Inspector? Coffee? Tea? Murderer?

NICK
Here is the murder weapon, Inspector. It's a little waterlogged, but I am sure the bullets will match the gun.

INSPECTOR
(takes gun and carefully puts it in his inside pocket)
On your feet, Mr. Trovimov.
Roughly grabs him, placing handcuffs over the sash.

INSPECTOR
Your sash, Madame.

He hands it back to her, tenderly.

INSPECTOR
As you Americans say, "It's the quiet ones you have to watch out for."
Mr. Smirnov, sorry for the misunderstanding. Just business.
(to PETER)
Let's go.

PETER turns and looks at ANYA.

PETER
Will you wait for me, my darling?

ANYA
In your dreams! And I hope I don't even bother showing up there. I hate
you, Peter, with every ounce of love I had for you, I hate you. I hope you
rot in hell!

ANYA runs upstairs. VARYA turns to go after her.

MME. RANEVSKAYA
Let her be.

VARYA
Good riddance to bad rubbish.

SIMON
Don't bother to write.

NORA
Goodbye, Peter... Nice meeting you!

*INSPECTOR leaves PETER with NICK for a moment, crosses to MME.
RANEVSKAYA, gently takes her hand and gazes tenderly into her eyes.
His words are heavy with meaning.*

INSPECTOR
I hope the next time I call on the Ranevskaya's, it will be a social call.
Do Skorogo.

*NICK walks him out into the awaiting car. There is a moment of silence.
The girls are smirking. MME. RANEVSKAYA is a little stunned, but
breaks into a smile as well.*

VARYA
Poor Gregor.
(pause)
Oh well!
(goes over to SIMON and kisses him)
First things first.

VARYA goes to the bookshelf and removes the picture of Yepikov.

VARYA
I guess we can hang this in the cottage bathroom, in memoriam. I sure
hope he doesn't haunt the place.

SIMON
I say we tear down the cottages. All of them. And re-plant the cherry
trees. It may take a while, but we have the rest of our lives. Does that
sound all right to you, MME. Ranevskaya?

MME. RANEVSKAYA
It sounds fine... Son.

VARYA
And of course, we want you to stay here with us, Mama, don't we,
Simon?

SIMON
It would be an honor, MME. Ranevskaya. Oh, Nora... How can we ever
thank you?

NORA
Just send us a case of your cherry vodka when your orchard blooms.
(hugs him)

NICK enters.

NICK
Well, that's the last you'll see of him for 20 or 30 years. Darling, I think
you should go upstairs and pack our bags. I owe you a shopping trip.

NORA
My new hat! Oh, Nicky!
(kisses him and runs upstairs)

NICK pours himself another drink.

NORA
(from upstairs)
Aren't you packing too, dear?

NICK
Yes, just putting away this liquor.
(takes a drink)

SIMON
Take the bottle, Mr. Charles. It's the least we can do.

MME. RANEVSKAYA
Mr. Charles, I know I haven't been very hospitable. I need to apologize.

NICK
Apology accepted, MME. Ranevskaya. Care for a drink?

MME. RANEVSKAYA
Thank you. I do believe this calls for a toast.
(everyone else gets a glass)
To you, Mr. Charles.
(everyone ad libs, "Here, here," etc.)
From the entire Ranevskaya family, I wish to express my gratitude. You
saved the lives of both my daughters. I can rest easy knowing Varya is in
good hands, and my sweet Anya has been released from the clutches of
that fiendish swine. The Ranevskayas are home at last. Where we
belong!

They all drink.

SIMON
There's still the question of money, though... upkeep...

VARYA
I was thinking... I could cook, get a little bakery business going. Varya's
Vatrushka, Ranevskaya's Rhubarb Pies, and I'm sure there is a market for
your cherry vodka, Simon.

NICK
Most definitely a market. I can connect you with some international
distributors. The Mrs. and I would certainly consider underwriting initial
business expenses in exchange for a few, uh... perks. I have no doubt this
will be the next big thing in alcohol.

NORA enters with a suitcase, wearing NICK's coat and hat.

NORA
I thought you were the biggest thing in alcohol, darling. Your suitcase is
rattling.

NICK
May I?

He takes his coat, opens his suitcase, which is filled with bottles, wraps his coat around the bottles and closes the suitcase.

NORA
You certainly are an efficient packer.

NICK
Years of practice.
(runs up to get the other suitcase)
Did you phone for a taxi?

NORA
I did. Our driver will be here shortly

MME. RANEVSKAYA hugs NORA.

MME. RANEVSKAYA
Thank you, my dear child. For everything.

VARYA hugs NORA.

VARYA
Come back anytime. Always consider this your home.

NORA
I think this is the beginning of a beautiful friendship.

ANYA comes downstairs with her suitcase.

MME. RANEVSKAYA
Anya? What's going on?

VARYA
You're not leaving, are you? You just got here.

ANYA

Oh, Mama, Varya, I am so happy for you both, but there is nothing for me here right now. I need to follow my own dreams. Nick, Nora, if I may, I'd like to accompany you back to New York. I want to be... an actress! I've always wanted that, but I've been too afraid.

MME. RANEVSKAYA

A daughter of mine? Alone in New York City?

NORA

Oh, she won't be alone. You can stay with us, dear, for as long as you want. We have plenty of room and I'm sure you'll find acting work in no time. How hard could it be?

NICK

(takes a drink)

The main thing is sincerity. If you can fake that, you've got it made.

MME. RANEVSKAYA

But do you even know if you can act?

ANYA

I fooled Peter, didn't I?

(pulls out the book)

With a few minor changes, these could be a hilarious comedy. Oh, Mama, I appreciate everything you've done for me. You have sacrificed so much for all of us. It's time for me to spread my wings, and time for you to enjoy life at last, here in your cherry orchard. Everything was here, your youth, your happiness, your memories, good and bad, but we need them all, Mama. How can we appreciate the good without having the bad to compare it to? I love you, Mama. Be happy!

(hugs her)

Car horn beeps.

MME. RANEVSKAYA

My dear, dear child. My odd duck has become a swan.

ANYA
I'm not a swan. I am... A SEAGULL!

ANYA grabs her suitcase and exits. NICK begins coughing.

NORA
Nicky! You OK?

NICK
I accidentally drank water by mistake. It went down the wrong way.
Anya will be fine, MME. Ranevskaya. We will see to that. My darling,
your new hat awaits you.

NORA
I love you, Nicky. I don't care what they all say. Goodbye, all.

NICK
We're coming home, Asta! I think I hear a martini being stirred.

*NICK and NORA exit. MME. RANEVSKAYA takes a moment, looking at
her surroundings. She goes to the back door to the cherry orchard and
breathes deeply.*

VARYA
Mama, you're crying.

MME. RANEVSKAYA
Spring will come. This home will be filled with life again. Life, love,
happiness, and in time, hopefully the laughter of children.

*MME. RANEVSKAYA does not see VARYA and SIMON's eyes widen in
terror at this suggestion, but we do. They quickly recover.*

MME. RANEVSKAYA (cont.)
Our suffering was not in vain. The sunlight is so beautiful on the
treetops. We have a roof of our own and a place by the fire.

VARYA

Fate is an unpredictable teacher, Mama. Come, let's have some tea.

VARYA takes her hand and they all start to exit. As the lights fade, MME. Ranevskaya grabs the bottle of vodka and brings it along.

FADE TO BLACK

END OF PLAY

Suggested curtain call music: Jack Hylton - Life is Just a Bowl of Cherries (1931) - reprise.

ABOUT THE AUTHOR

Bambi Everson is a playwright, actress, and teaching artist. She studied with Geraldine Page and Michael Schulman, and appeared in many Off-Off Broadway productions in her youth. She wrote her first play in 2015, and has since completed over 20 more, including six full-lengths.

Her work tends to incorporate oddball characters and situations, from screwball comedy to dark melodrama, from cannibals in suburban Long Island, to murderous love triangles amongst octogenarians in an assisted living facility. She's been influenced as much by cinema as she has by theater, an inescapable accident of birth, as she's the daughter of noted film historian, William K. Everson.

Her work has been produced at Manhattan Repertory Theatre, Hudson Guild, Emerging Artists Theatre and The Little Theatre of Alexandria, VA, and college productions in North Carolina and Arkansas. THE THIN MAN IN THE CHERRY ORCHARD was featured at the 2019 New York Fringe Festival. She was the recipient of the 2015 Yip Harburg Foundation award. She teaches playwriting at PPAS in Manhattan, and is a member of The Dramatist's Guild.

Follow her adventures at her website, bambieverson.com.

More plays by Bambi Everson

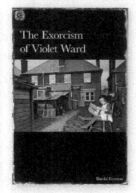

Visit BambiEverson.com

CPSIA information can be obtained
at www.ICGtesting.com
Printed in the USA
LVHW021603030921
696794LV00015B/1918